How to Think and Intervene Like a Single-Session Therapist

Therapists new to Single-Session Therapy (SST) will often struggle to bring the SST mindset to the work and will in turn struggle to help their clients get the most out of the time that they choose to spend together.

How to Think and Intervene Like a Single-Session Therapist provides the trainee with an opportunity to discover how experienced therapists think, and how their thoughts influence their interventions within the single-session context. Presenting SST in a way that both interests conventional therapists and shows the potential of this way of delivering therapy services, Windy Dryden details the multiple levels of thinking and intervening that go into single-session practice. He covers the orientation thinking experienced SST therapists have about the work when they are not doing it, the pre-session thinking they engage in while actively preparing to do the work, and the in-session thinking they engage in while doing the work. The book outlines the theory behind SST and the ways those ideas form its practice, using clinical vignettes and case scenarios to demonstrate how single-session therapists can make the best use of the limited time with their clients. The book additionally presents an ongoing dialogue between an SST therapist and a conventional therapist to highlight the thinking of the former and how the criticisms of SST by the latter can be responded to.

This highly practical guide will be essential reading for any therapist who is new to or has recently been introduced to the practice of SST.

Windy Dryden is in clinical and consultative practice and is an international authority on Single-Session Therapy. He is Emeritus Professor of Psychotherapeutic Studies at Goldsmiths, University of London. He has worked in psychotherapy for more than 45 years and is the author or editor of over 275 books.

How to Think and Intervene Like a Single-Session Therapist

Windy Dryden

Routledge
Taylor & Francis Group

LONDON AND NEW YORK

First published 2024
by Routledge
4 Park Square, Milton Park, Abingdon, Oxon OX14 4RN

and by Routledge
605 Third Avenue, New York, NY 10158

Routledge is an imprint of the Taylor & Francis Group, an informa business

British Library Cataloguing-in-Publication Data
A catalogue record for this book is available from the British Library

ISBN: 9781032657363 (hbk)
ISBN: 9781032657356 (pbk)
ISBN: 9781032657752 (ebk)

DOI: 10.4324/9781032657752

Typeset in Times New Roman
by Newgen Publishing UK

Contents

Introduction   1

PART I
SST 'Orientation' Thinking   3

1   One Session or More – Be Open to Both Possibilities   5

2   Help at the Point of Need   9

3   It Is Possible to Conduct a Session in SST
    without Prior Knowledge of the Person   16

4   View the Session as a Whole, Complete in Itself   20

5   Potentially Anyone Can Be Helped in a Single
    Session   25

6   Focus on the Person, Not the Disorder   29

7   The Client–Therapist Relationship Can Be
    Established Rapidly   33

8   SST Is Client-Led   38

9   The Power of Now   44

10 Less Is More   48

11 Take Nothing for Granted   50

PART II
SST 'Pre-Session' Thinking   53

12 Informing Potential Clients about SST   55

13 Responding to Potential Clients' Questions
    about SST   60

14 Eliciting Informed Consent from Clients   65

15 Helping Clients to Prepare for the Session   68

16 Preparing Oneself for the Session   74

PART III
SST 'In-Session' Thinking   81

17 Beginning the Session   83

18 Helping the Client to Nominate a Goal   93

19 Discovering What Help the Client Is Seeking
    from the Therapist   96

20 Creating a Focus and Maintaining It   103

21 Understanding the Problem   108

22 Searching for a Solution   127

23 Embedding the Solution   148

24 Encouraging the Client to Rehearse the Solution   150

25 Helping the Client to Develop and Implement
      an Action Plan   156

26 Ending the Session   163

Afterword: After the Session   168

Appendix 1: Therapeutic Contract with
      Professor Windy Dryden: ONEplus Therapy   *171*
Appendix 2: ONEplus Therapy Session
      Rating Scale   *173*
Appendix 3: Follow-Up Telephone Evaluation
      Protocol   *175*
References   *179*
Index   *182*

Introduction

In 2003, I read *Single Session Therapy: Maximizing the Effect of the First (and Often Only) Therapeutic Encounter* by Moshe Talmon (1990). While I found it interesting, I did not resonate with the ideas Talmon expounded. Looking back, I realised I had read the book from a conventional therapy mindset. When I re-read the book ten years later, I was much more open to what Talmon had to say. In the intervening years, I had carried out many single-session therapy demonstrations at training workshops and became interested in what was possible to achieve in a therapeutic relationship in a very brief period.

At around that time, I retired from my university position and was looking for a new challenge in the twilight of my career in psychotherapy. Inspired by my second reading of Talmon's book, I devoted my time to doing single-session therapy (SST) and training counsellors and therapists in its practice. Another decade on, having run over a hundred short- and longer-term training events on SST and having written several books on the subject (e.g., Dryden, 2020, 2021), my view is that the heart of the single-session way of working with people is the thinking that therapist has about SST and which describes their orientation to the work (which I call SST 'orientation' thinking), the thinking they engage in while actively preparing to do the work (which I call SST 'pre-session' thinking) and the thinking that they engage in while doing the work (which I call SST 'in-session' thinking). These three types of thinking comprise the single-session mindset (Cannistrà, 2022). This mindset orients the therapist to the work and influences their clinical decisions and what they do in practice.

Unless therapists new to SST bring the SST mindset to the work and think like an SST therapist while doing the work, then they will struggle to help their clients get the most out of the time that they

DOI: 10.4324/9781032657752-1

choose to spend together. It is for this reason that I decided to write this book.

In a previous volume (Dryden, 2024a), I wrote about how therapists new to Rational Emotive Behaviour Therapy (REBT) could learn how to practise REBT by studying the in-session thinking experienced REBT therapists engage in and how they intervene with their clients based on this thinking. In addition, I compared the in-session thinking of these trained REBT therapists with that engaged in by trainee REBT therapists. The contrast between the two would highlight what the trainee REBT could aspire to.

In this book, I have retained the essence of the REBT volume by focusing on how the SST therapist thinks and intervenes while practising SST. I will detail the thinking experienced SST therapists have about the work when they not doing it and which describes their orientation to the work, the pre-session thinking they engage in while actively preparing to do the work and the in-session thinking they engage in while doing the work. However, given that SST offers a challenge to practitioners of more conventional therapy, I decided to construct an ongoing dialogue between an SST therapist and a conventional therapist[1] to highlight the thinking of the former and how the criticisms of SST by the latter can be responded to.

My explicit intention is to present SST in a way that both interests conventional therapists and shows the potential of this way of delivering therapy services. The way I have chosen to write the book means I will outline SST and the ideas that inform its practice along the way rather than beginning the book with this material.

Unlike REBT, single-session therapy is not an approach to therapy. Instead, it is a way of delivering therapy based on a particular way of thinking about therapy. Given this, therapists can practice SST from various therapy approaches. This means that what I will do in this book is present ideas generally accepted in the SST community while recognising that different therapists will sometimes practise SST in different ways.

Windy Dryden
London, Eastbourne
June, 2023

---

1 Given that SST therapists can practise conventional therapy and conventional therapists can practise SST, the constructed dialogue is really between a therapist articulating the SST mindset and a therapist critical of that mindset because they are viewing SST from a conventional therapy mindset.

Part I

SST 'Orientation' Thinking

In the Introduction, I distinguished between three types of SST thinking comprising the SST mindset: SST 'orientation' thinking, SST 'pre-session' thinking and SST 'in-session' thinking. SST 'orientation' thinking is the general thinking the SST therapist engages in when they are reflecting on the work and describes their orientation *to* the work. Such thinking is neither directly concerned with the active preparations the therapist makes before doing SST, nor is it concerned with how the therapist works with a particular client. On the other hand, SST 'pre-session thinking' is the thinking in which the therapist engages as they *actively prepare* to do the work and 'in-session' thinking is the thinking in which the SST therapist engages *in* during the session. It is more specific and directly concerned with how to help the client the therapist is working with.

In this first part of the book, I will focus on SST 'orientation' thinking.

DOI: 10.4324/9781032657752-2

Chapter 1

One Session or More – Be Open to Both Possibilities

When therapists with a conventional mindset are first introduced to single-session therapy (SST), understandably, perhaps, they think that this is a therapy that lasts for a single session with no further help being offered. As such, they find it difficult to fathom how it is possible to help a person in that restricted period. In making this judgment, these therapists are making two false assumptions. First, they assume that SST only involves a single session which, as we will see presently, is not the case. Second, by 'help', they have a different concept in mind than do SST therapists. For a conventional therapist to have helped someone, that person must have reached a criterion set by the therapist or therapeutic community. For example, in a review of the outcome of psychological treatment carried out in 32 IAPT[1] services, Gyani, Shafran, Layard and Clark (2013: 599) said that 'patients were deemed to have reliably recovered if they scored above the clinical cut-off on the PHQ-9 and/or the GAD-7[2] at initial assessment, they showed reliable improvement during treatment, and they scored below the clinical cut-offs on *both* the PHQ-9 and the GAD-7 at the end of treatment.' In this conventional view, therapy represents the end of something. In contrast, SST therapy represents the beginning of a process that the client may choose to continue on their own or with further therapeutic help.

---

1 IAPT stands for 'Improving Access to the Psychological Therapies'. It is a UK National Health Service initiative to provide more psychotherapy to the general population. In 2023 it was rebranded as 'NHS Talking Therapies, for anxiety and depression.'

2 The Patient Health Questionnaire-9 (PHQ-9) and Generalised Anxiety Disorder-7 (GAD-7) are short screening measures used in medical and community settings to assess depression and anxiety severity.

DOI: 10.4324/9781032657752-3

What Is Single-Session Therapy?

I have defined single-session therapy thus:

Single-session therapy is a purposeful endeavour where both therapist and client make a contract based on informed consent to work together to help the client in one session to achieve their stated wants on the understanding that more help is available if needed (Dryden, 2021a).

The critical elements of this definition are as follows:

- Both client and therapist make a contract based on understanding what SST is and what it can and probably can't do.
- The purpose of SST is to help the client, if possible, to achieve their stated wants in one session. Its intent should ideally *not* be to help agencies or independent practitioners reduce waiting lists and waiting times. While the *consequence* of SST is that it does bring down such lists and waiting times for an appointment in services where SST is by appointment, this is not the purpose of SST. Its purpose is as stated above.
- SST does not provide a barrier to further help should the client request this. It may well be that they are happy with what they have taken away from the single session. Still, it is vital that they understand that they can access further help, assuming that this is available from the relevant agencies or independent practitioners. If it is not available, a judicial referral should be effected. If the client is offered further help by the agency or independent practitioner concerned, they need to know how long it will take for this help to become available.
- Thus, the SST therapist combines two seemingly different positions: to help the client in one session and provide further help if requested.

Having made the point that the SST therapist integrates the 'no further help is needed' and 'further help is needed' positions, they must be even-handed in holding these positions when working with a client and do so throughout the first and perhaps only session they will have with the client. This is where implicit bias may take place. For example, a therapist new to SST who is working with a client and 'hears' that the client has more issues that they have tabled for discussion in the session may suggest to the client that they may need extra sessions to deal with these issues even though the client has not expressed such a wish. On the other hand, an SST therapist may consider it a failure if a client wishes to have further help and may implicitly discourage them from requesting it even though that would be an appropriate request.

Let's pick up on the dialogue between an SST therapist and a conventional therapist on this point.

Conventional therapist: I understand that in single-session therapy, you don't restrict your client from having more sessions, but surely if someone has signed up for single-session therapy, they implicitly feel that they can't have any more help and they would be a failure should they request it.

Single-session therapist: Yes, that would be a concern. However, a good SST therapist is primarily concerned with the person getting the help that they think they need. So, although they have both agreed to work together to see if they can help the client take away what the client has come for at the end of the session, the therapist would be clear that it is equally OK for the person to request further help.

Conventional therapist: But many clients need more help even if they don't realise that they do.

Single-session therapist: You have hit on a fundamental issue. In single-session therapy, we are clear that the client determines their therapy agenda and decides to have one or more therapy sessions. In conventional therapy, the therapist is seen to be the expert and guides such treatment decisions. I will discuss this issue further later.

In my supervision of therapists new to SST, I realise that this is one of the frustrations of doing SST work – not providing the help that the therapist thinks the client needs rather than trusting the client to be the best judge of what they want to seek help for and how much help they want.

In closing, let me consider the issue of what to call this mode of therapy delivery. It is widely known as 'single-session therapy'. However, I have found that no matter how often I stress that this does not mean that the client is restricted to one session, the term 'single-session therapy' does seem to leave an indelible impression that this is the case. There are two alternatives to the term 'single-session therapy'.

The first is known as 'One-At-A-Time' therapy (OAATT). This is a term Michael Hoyt (2011) put forward as a synonym for single-session therapy. This term has been used widely in university and college counselling services where a client can have another session after the first but can only request it after a period of two weeks, for example. So, a client can have several sessions but can only have them one session at a time with a two-week gap between sessions.

The second is a term that I use to describe my single-session work. It is 'ONEplus therapy'. I have capitalised the word 'ONE' because it indicates that it is a principal objective of this way of working to help the person with what they have come for by the end of the session. The word 'plus' is attached to the word 'ONE' without a space to indicate that more help is available to the client on request and that this is an integral part of the delivery mode. Unlike 'One-At-A-Time therapy', 'ONEplus therapy' does not restrict *when* the person can access further help should they decide to do so. Also, the person can access any form of therapy delivery offered by the agency or independent practitioner. If they request a form of help not provided by the above, then, if possible, a suitable external referral is made.

In addition, given the dual nature of this way of working ('let's help you in one session/more help is available'), the term 'ONEplus therapy' does not suggest that only one session is offered to the client, which, in the minds of many, is suggested by the term 'single-session therapy'. See Dryden (2023a) for more information on ONEplus therapy.

Chapter 2

Help at the Point of Need

Introduction

In almost all cases, therapists enter the profession to help people seeking therapeutic services as quickly as possible. Very few would say, 'I prefer to see clients who have been on a lengthy waiting list rather than to do so straight away.' And yet, the norm is that clients are generally seen after a lengthy wait.

I once read of a therapy agency being lauded for its excellent work providing therapy for clients who have psychological difficulties but who present with physical symptoms. This service was staffed by therapists from a broad range of therapeutic approaches. However, the therapy service manager admitted that those referred to the agency had to wait longer than 18 months for an appointment. I am not in any way questioning the quality of therapy offered by this agency. What struck me was the juxtaposition between the agency being put forward as an excellent example of how the NHS can offer psychotherapy and the length of time clients had to wait to be seen.

When discussing their own waiting lists, therapists in independent practice often hold two attitudes – one explicit, the other implicit. Their explicit attitude is to decry the length of time people have to wait to be seen. 'I wish I could see people more quickly' is the oft-heard claim by this group. If they similarly voiced their implicit attitude, it would be, 'Look how good I am. People have to wait a long time to see me'. Indeed, some research shows that consumers value a product more if they wait for it (Giebelhausen, Robinson & Cronin, 2011). However, therapists rarely admit this implicit attitude explicitly and certainly not in a professional gathering. I am saying that therapists

DOI: 10.4324/9781032657752-4

may be ambivalent about clients waiting for their services. As shown above, part of them decries this state of affairs, while another part sees the positive in it for their professional self-esteem.

From a different perspective, qualitative data from students in universities where One-At-A-Time therapy services have been introduced show that many students appreciate being seen quickly and at the time of their choosing.

Help at the Point of Need: The SST Viewpoint

We know little about what happens before a person decides to seek therapeutic help. It is likely, however, that a person will have attempted to help themself before reaching out for professional help. The help at the point of need principle states that this person should be offered the opportunity to begin therapy as quickly as possible after they have made that initial approach.

The practice of SST closely aligns with the 'help at the point of need' principle. Indeed, a significant context in which SST is practised is in open-access, walk-in[1] centres where, as the name makes clear, people can access a single session of therapy by accessing such a centre at a time of their choosing, and nobody is turned away.[2]

However, in the United Kingdom, SST is more likely to be practised where clients have to make an appointment to access a therapy service rather than to use an agency that provides immediately available help.[3] In the UK, the usual practice in an appointment-based system is that the client is given an initial appointment where a representative of that agency assesses them to determine what help the agency thinks the person needs. There is usually a wait for such an

---

1 There are two problems with the term 'walk-in'. First, not everybody can walk. Suppose someone has a disability and wants to access therapy provided by a 'walk-in' centre. In that case, it is hopefully clear that their inability to 'walk into' the service is not a barrier. Second, increasingly, SST takes place online or digitally, where there is no physical space to walk into. The term 'open access' is an excellent alternative with two components: a) it clarifies that a person can access the service whenever it is open, b) it is open to everyone. As an alternative term I will refer to 'open-access, enter now' services.

2 I will discuss this latter point more extensively later in this book.

3 When I say 'immediate', here, I am not saying that the person is seen the moment they arrive at an 'open-access, enter now' facility, as there is usually a short wait. By immediate, I mean that they will be seen on that same visit.

assessment appointment. Then after the person has been assigned to a particular form of help determined by the agency, there is another wait for a therapy appointment to be offered. At that first therapy appointment, the treating therapist will likely assess the patient in a more detailed manner than at the previous assessment session, take a case history, and/or conduct a case formulation. Then therapy will begin.

The contrast between this and help provided at the point of need in an 'open-access, enter now' facility is clear. But what happens when an agency offers SST by appointment? Ideally, the person will have decided to access SST based on information provided on the agency's website or by an agency representative whose initial task is *not* to assess the suitability of clients for different forms of therapy delivery but to clarify for the person what services are available and have the person decide which form of therapy delivery best meets their current needs. In my view, once the person has reached out for an SST appointment, they should be given one no later than a week after their initial contact. Otherwise, the therapeutic potency of SST will be diluted. It certainly makes no sense to put a person on a lengthy waiting list for SST.

The Principles of Help at the Point of Need

The term 'help at the point of need' clearly describes the situation where a person is given help at the point of their need rather than at the point of appointment availability on the part of an agency or an independent practitioner. Several other principles of 'help at the point of need' are relevant to the practice of SST and which SST therapists bring to this practice.

Some Help Now Is Better than Full Help Much Later Unless the Client Chooses to Wait

Many conventional therapists believe there should be empirically supported treatments for various mental health conditions. It follows that it is important for the client to be assessed correctly so that the proper treatment can be provided. From this perspective, single-session therapy would make no sense as assessing the person and treating them thoroughly in a single session would not be possible. The SST therapist's thinking that they bring to the work is very different on this issue. Here the focus is not on mental health conditions that need to be assessed but on the client's stated wants from the session that need to be met if possible. Given that SST can be accessed more quickly than a protocol-driven treatment for an assessed mental health condition, SST thinking is that it is better for the person to access immediate help than wait for the protocol-driven treatment to become available. However, given that privileging the client's view is an important value in SST, if the client chooses to wait for the protocol-driven treatment and not access SST, that is fine.

Providing Immediate Help Is More Important than Carrying Out a Full Assessment and/or a Case Formulation

SST is predicated on the finding that the modal number[4] of sessions clients have in a therapy agency is '1', followed by '2', followed by '3', etc. This finding is universal (see Brown & Jones, 2005; Hoyt & Talmon, 2014; Young, 2018). We also do not know which clients will have one session and which clients will have more. The SST therapist's thinking about such data is as follows: given that we do not know how many sessions a given client will have, let us immediately provide them with the help they want rather than assessing them for help that we think they may need and which they will be provided with later, sometimes much later.

Again, it may be that a client wants a more conventional approach to therapy, and if they are prepared to wait for it, OK. If so, the therapist may carry out a full assessment and/or case formulation. However, to attempt to carry out these activities in SST would be foolhardy as they take far more time than the therapist and client have contracted for.

---

4 The mode represents the most frequently occurring number in a series. It is very different from the mean. Consider a situation where nine clients in an agency each have one session and the tenth has 100 sessions. The mode here is '1', and the mean is 10.9. When I am invited to give an SST training workshop for an agency, I ask for the modal number of sessions that clients have, but I am often given the mean instead. When I push for the latter, it is clear that the agency has not appreciated the importance of modal data.

Therapy Can Be Initiated in the Absence of a Case History

While taking a case history from a client may be a valuable exercise in conventional therapy, again, doing so is not a good way of spending time in SST. However, I tend to ask, 'What do you think I need to know about your history that if I didn't know, would mean that I could not help you?' This allows the client to focus and, if necessary, identify a factor that I will make use of if I can during the session.

People Have the Resources to Make Use of Help Provided at the Point of Need

If people did not have the resources to benefit from SST, then SST would not have developed as broadly as it has. Human beings often surprise themselves with their achievements from a single-session conversation. This does not mean that they can change themselves radically in an hour. Instead, they can take something valuable from the session and choose to implement this going forward.

The Best Way to See if a Client Will Benefit from SST Is to Offer Them SST, Engage Them in the Process and See How They Respond

As mentioned earlier, one of the core SST ideas that conventional therapists struggle with is that SST therapists offer clients therapy from the outset without engaging them in prior activities such as person-based assessment, case history taking or case formulation. How, they argue, can you judge if someone is suitable for SST if you don't engage the person in some form of pre-therapy assessment? The SST response is the best way of discovering if a client will benefit from SST is to offer them SST, and if they accept, engage them in the process and see if they benefit from it at the end of the session.

Therapy Can Be Initiated Straightaway, and Risk Can Be Managed if This Becomes an Issue

Conventional therapists express a similar concern about managing risk. Surely, they argue, you need to manage risk before engaging the person in therapy. Otherwise, you may open up a can of worms that you can't close by the end of the session. SST therapists respond by arguing that if it is discovered that a person is at risk during the session, it is dealt with as it would be in any other mode of therapy delivery. As such, a good outcome from the session would be to help the client develop a plan to keep them safe from harm. Also, the risk of 'opening up a can of worms' would be minimised because a) both client and therapist would be clear about what SST can and can't do, b) therapy would be focused on the client's stated wants from the session and c) the therapist would work to keep the client's feelings contained.

The Client Best Determines the Length of Therapy

Providing help at the point of client need means that the client's issues are dealt with quickly, and as such, the person may not stay in therapy for very long. This usually does not sit well with the conventional therapist, who may believe that longer-term therapy is needed to help the person deal with all their issues. However, the client may not want all their issues dealt with and are happy to leave if they have gotten what they have come for. They decide how many sessions they will have, their therapist doesn't.

Let's pick up on the dialogue between an SST therapist and a conventional therapist on this point.

Conventional therapist: I like the idea of helping a client at the point of their need, but I am uncomfortable beginning therapy from what you call 'moment one'. Why can't I help a client at the point of their need and do a case formulation, for example? In my training, I have been taught not to start therapy without doing a case formulation.

Single-session therapist: Of course, you can begin therapy by doing a case formulation or anything else you deem important before initiating therapy. However, in SST, we are guided by the finding that the modal number of sessions clients have in agency-based therapy is '1'. This means that it is quite likely that the person in front of you will only attend once. They may attend many more sessions, but the point is that you don't know. Consequently, if you bring a single-session mindset to the first session, you will be guided by the point that you may never see the person again and as such, you will ask yourself the question, how do I want to spend the time that I *know* I have with this person? Your answer will be, 'to give them a session of therapy focused on their stated wants'.

While you are attracted to a part of the single-session mindset – helping a client at the point of their need – you have an issue with the practical implications of this, which is beginning therapy from moment one. This seems to conflict with your conventional therapy mindset. I would suggest that you conduct an experiment. See ten clients for SST, begin therapy from moment one with five of them and with the other five, begin by doing a case formulation and then begin therapy. Review the findings at the end of the experiment.

Chapter 3

It Is Possible to Conduct a Session in SST without Prior Knowledge of the Person

The development of what I refer to in this book as SST 'orientation' thinking, SST 'pre-session thinking' and SST 'in-session' thinking that comprise the SST mindset stems from the experiences of those therapists who have worked in 'open-access, enter now' therapy centres. When somebody accesses help at such a centre, they may be asked for minimal biographical information. Here, the therapist is effectively being asked to do therapy with someone they know virtually nothing about. Some conventional therapists may be nervous about doing this, but it isn't a barrier to effective therapy in the aforementioned 'open-access, enter now' centres. If that is the case, it is also possible that single-session therapists can work with clients in agencies that offer SST by appointment without prior knowledge of them.

As I will discuss later in the book, most SST therapists capitalise on the time between a client making an appointment and the appointment taking place by inviting the client to complete a pre-session questionnaire, the purpose of which is to encourage the client to prepare for the session so that they can get the most out of it. The client who completes the questionnaire is invited to return it to their therapist so that the latter can prepare themself for the session.

The questions on the questionnaire are centred on the following:

- The issue that the client wishes to discuss with the therapist.
- What the client has already done to deal with the issue and the outcome of these attempts.
- The internal resources that the client can bring to the session as the two of them work with the issue and as the client implements takeaways after the session.
- The external resources that the client can call upon as they strive to implement their takeaways after the session.

DOI: 10.4324/9781032657752-5

- The type of help the client is looking for from the therapist (see Chapter 19).
- Anything else the client thinks the therapist needs to know to help the client with the issue.

As I mentioned above, the client is invited, not mandated to complete and return the questionnaire. If they don't, the therapist will still see them and may use some of the questions to begin the session.

Occasionally, a client may complete and return the questionnaire to the therapist, but at the beginning of the session, they indicate that they wish to discuss a different issue to the one that they have written about on the questionnaire. It is important that the therapist is flexible enough to deal with the change and is not thrown by it.

I also know that some SST therapists prefer not to read a client's completed and returned questionnaire because they prefer to work with clients without knowing anything about them. They argue that they want to work with what the client wants to focus on *now* rather than be guided by what the client wrote a few days ago. These therapists see the pre-session questionnaire as an opportunity for the *client* to prepare for the session. *They* will prepare for the session by getting into the spirit of SST 'pre-session' thinking rather than by being informed by the client's reflections on what they want to gain from the session, which may be out of date by the time the single session happens. Such therapists have a surprising ally in Wilfred Bion (1967: 272), the psychoanalyst, who said, '[e]very session attended by the psychoanalyst must have no history and no future'.

A good illustration of what this group of SST therapists is concerned with occurred with a therapist whom I was supervising. The therapist worked in an agency that had introduced SST as a therapy delivery option for clients. The therapist was due to see the client on Monday morning and received the person's pre-therapy questionnaire on Friday afternoon. Reading the client's responses, the therapist discovered that the client's nominated[1] issue for the session was problematic anger. The therapist had been trained to work with anxiety and depression but had no experience in working with anger.

---

1 I refer to the issue that the client is seeking help from the SST therapist as their 'nominated' issue.

Consequently, she spent the entire weekend learning about problematic anger and how to deal with it therapeutically. When she came to see the client on Monday morning, the client had changed their mind and wanted to work with an anxiety problem. While the therapist, in my view, needed to learn to work with anger, to spend an anxiety-filled weekend doing so was probably not the best learning environment. However, this is not the point. The point is that SST therapists need to be open to dealing with whatever clients want to bring to SST and don't need to know in advance about a particular client's nominated issue.

I have had experience in doing over 750 live demonstrations of SST in front of a primarily professional audience (Dryden, 2021b). I know nothing about a person who volunteers to be my client, except on certain occasions I know the problem area because the demonstration is taking place in the context of a training workshop on 'SST with "x"' where 'x' is the problem area (e.g., 'SST with anxiety' or 'SST with procrastination'). Other than that, I know nothing about the volunteer. Having no prior knowledge about a person has never proven an obstacle to my being able to help them (e.g., Dryden, 2018, 2021c).

Finally, suppose an SST therapist wants prior knowledge about the client. In that case, they can ask the person on the pre-session questionnaire or at the beginning of the session a question such as, 'From your perspective, what do you think I need to know about you as a person which, if I did not know, I would not be able to help you?' The response to this question tells the SST therapist what the client deems crucial for them to know. This question puts the client in charge of determining the vital nature of such information, not the therapist.

Let's pick up on the dialogue between an SST and a conventional therapist on this point.

Conventional therapist: I work in an agency which receives referrals where a lot is known about the client before we see them. We find this very useful in helping us to determine what the person needs therapeutically. We would find it difficult to do without this information.

SST therapist: I understand that this information is very useful in helping your agency determine the right therapy for a person, and I am not suggesting that you change this thinking or the practice that stems from it. However, this type of thinking won't work if you want to introduce SST as a form of therapy delivery into your agency. There are a number of ways of incorporating SST into your agency's service delivery.

If you want to preserve the practice that you mentioned above where you get referrals with a lot of accompanying information about the people referred, then, probably the best way of introducing SST into your agency is as a service that runs alongside these other forms of therapy delivery and allows clients who want to access SST to do so. This will preserve the principle of client self-determination that is at the heart of SST and enable clients to be seen quickly. There is no value to be gained from getting the same information about clients who opt for SST as you get about clients who you may wish to refer to the agency's services. Indeed, there is much to lose as the process takes time and the longer it takes a client to access SST the more SST will lose its therapeutic potency.

Chapter 4

View the Session as a Whole, Complete in Itself

A while ago, a good friend asked me to look at a draft of a book he was writing on psychotherapy. In that book, he made the following statement that stood out for me: 'The purpose of the first session in psychotherapy is to get the person to come back for the second session'. Now that may make sense if one adopts a conventional therapy mindset, but it is not a useful way of thinking about SST. The SST 'orientation' thinking version of my friend's statement is as follows: 'The purpose of the first session in psychotherapy is for the therapist to work with the client so that the client does not need to come back for the second. However, if the client wants a second session, then that is fine too'.

The First Session in Conventional Therapy

As I discussed in Chapter 2, the first session in conventional therapy tends to be devoted to some or all of the following activities:

- contracting;
- discussion of treatment expectations;
- person-based assessment;
- history taking;
- case formulation;
- rapport building;
- discussion of the client's outcome goals for therapy; and
- having the client tell their story in their own way.

While these activities may have therapeutic value for the client, they are best seen as a precursor to psychotherapy rather than an integral part of psychotherapy itself. The American Psychological Association uses the following definition. 'Psychotherapy is the informed and

DOI: 10.4324/9781032657752-6

intentional application of clinical methods and interpersonal stances derived from established psychological principles for the purpose of assisting people to modify their behaviors, cognitions, emotions, and/or other personal characteristics in directions that the participants deem desirable' (Campbell, Norcross, Vasquez & Kaslow, 2013).

Given that the aforementioned activities are best seen as a precursor to psychotherapy, it follows from this perspective, that the first session is viewed as a part of a longer process, As I said earlier, this is very much how a conventional therapist regards the first therapy session.

By contrast, the SST therapist views the first session as complete in itself because they know that there is a reasonably good chance that this session may be the only session that the client will attend. This is neatly summed up in the title of Moshe Talmon's (1990) pioneering book, 'Single Session Therapy: Maximizing the Effect of the First (and Often Only) Therapeutic Encounter.' If the client requests more help, this may be at the end of the session, it may be after an agreed time when they reflect on the session, digest what they learned from it, implement any takeaways and see what happens before making a decision about seeking further help. And, of course, it may be that the person has gotten what they came for and doesn't need any more help. As we have seen this is the most likely outcome in agencies, even where SST is not a planned form of service delivery. When it is planned then, about 50% of clients are satisfied with the help received from the session and request no further help at that time.

A conventional therapist looking at these figures would regard the 50% as drop-outs from treatment because their therapists have failed to engage them in therapy. Indeed, in the IAPT study mentioned in Chapter 1, they did not even include clients who only attended one session in their study because these clients were deemed not to have received a 'minimal dose' of therapy. This is what Gyani et al. (2013: 598) say: 'To be considered someone who had at least a minimal dose of therapy, patients had to have attended at least two sessions. This was because: 1) it was thought unlikely that patients who had only one session would have received a significant amount of treatment as the first session was almost always devoted to assessment'. This encapsulates the conventional therapy mindset: a) the first session is devoted to assessment; b) the first session is regarded as the precursor to what follows. Therefore, it is not complete in itself; and c) nothing of therapeutic benefit is expected to come from the first session if it is not followed by therapy. Clients who only attend the first assessment session are not even worthy of study since they are unlikely to have benefitted from the session.

Despite the fact that the modal number of sessions that clients have in such agencies is '1' as we have seen, certainly IAPT agencies at that time and to a large degree now in its present form as 'NHS Talking Therapies, anxiety and depression' provide a service to these people that they themselves do not think much of in terms of likely therapeutic benefit for the patient.[1]

The First (and Perhaps Only) Session in Single-Session Therapy: Its Process

Hoyt (2018) has outlined a process view of single-session therapy which shows how he views the session as a whole, complete in itself. Extrapolating from Hoyt's ideas, it is possible to see the session as comprising a number of sequential phases.

Phase 1: Before the Client and Therapist Agree to Work Together

There is an important phase of SST that occurs before the client and therapist agree to work with one another. Before the person becomes a client, they can be said to be occupying one or more help-related roles (Seabury, Seabury & Garvin, 2011). When they occupy the *explorer* role, the person has decided that they have an issue for which they want help and are exploring help-seeking possibilities. When they approach an agency or an independent practitioner with questions about the services that they offer (including SST), they occupy the *enquirer* role. On the basis of their exploration and the responses they get to their questions, they may be said to occupy the *applicant* role when they approach an agency or practitioner for help. They become a *client* when they have given their informed consent to proceed.

---

1   I was involved in a pilot study where SST was introduced as a service in one IAPT agency. However, the agency followed the traditional model of devoting the first contact to assessment and thus clients were assessed for their suitability for SST rather than deciding for themselves whether to access SST. Perhaps unsurprisingly only clients with minor symptoms were referred to SST. This is what happens when SST is offered within an agency where conventional therapy thinking predominates.

Phase 2: The Pre-Session Preparation Phase

When SST is offered by appointment, there is a short period of time between when an appointment is made and when that appointment takes place.[2] Taking advantage of this time period is a key feature of SST 'pre-session' thinking. This feature espouses the value of time being used well during the SST process.[3]

The most common way of asking clients to prepare for the session is by questionnaire. What I recommend is that the therapist who will be seeing the client emails that client, introduces themself and gives the client a rationale for them to complete the questionnaire; namely that it will help them to prepare for the session so that they get the most from it. I also recommend that the therapist stresses the voluntary nature of the client completing the form. Finally, the client is invited to return the completed form to the therapist so that the latter can also prepare for the session. I will discuss this issue more fully in Chapter 15.

Phase 3: Beginning the Session

After the formalities of contracting have been completed, the main task of the SST therapist in the beginning phase of the session is to develop a good working alliance with the client quickly (see Chapter 7). This involves offering the kind of help the client is looking for (see Chapter 19), and what their session goal is (see Chapter 18). Knowing the latter, in particular helps the therapist identify a focus for the session with the client which helps both keep on track so that the client can walk away from the session with what they have come for.

Phase 4: The Middle Phase of the Session

Although different clients request different forms of help from SST therapists, the most common request is for the therapist to help the

---

2 I believe the session should take place within a week of the person coming for SST. Otherwise, the therapeutic potency of SST becomes diluted. As mentioned in Chapter 2, it makes no sense to put people on a long waiting list for an SST appointment.

3 Even in 'open-access, enter now' centres, there is usually a period between when a client arrives and when they are seen by a therapist. In this period, the person can be invited to prepare for the session by completing a pre-session questionnaire in the same way as are clients attending an SST by appointment clinic.

client with an emotional/behavioural problem with which they are stuck. In this case, the therapist will assist them both to get to the heart of the issue and to identify a solution to this problem. Once found, the solution is rehearsed and fine-tuned and the two make plans for the client to put this solution into practice once obstacles to doing so have been identified and dealt with.

Phase 5: Ending the Session

At this point, the therapist asks the client to summarise the work, specify their take-aways and think about how they can generalise their learning. Then, the therapist deals with any unfinished business the client may have about what they have discussed. The client is then reminded that they can access further help if they need it and how they may do that before the session comes to an end.

Phase 6: Post-Session

After the session the client may be asked for immediate feedback on the session, contacted after a couple of weeks to see how they are going and whether or not they need further help and contacted again much later for feedback on outcome and what they thought of the service they received.

Let's pick up on the dialogue between an SST therapist and a conventional therapist on this point.

Conventional therapist: I am comfortable thinking of longer-term therapy as a process with a beginning, a middle and an end, but to see that a single session has a similar process is stretching a point.

Single-session therapist: I can imagine that it might be difficult, but I think if you practised SST from a single-session mindset you might begin to see the process nature of the work. If you don't practise SST, all you have is my word on the subject which you may be reluctant to take.

Chapter 5

Potentially Anyone Can Be Helped in a Single Session

When I first became interested in single-session therapy, and as I was developing my way of implementing this form of therapy delivery, I engaged with the question, 'Who is suitable for SST and who isn't?' As a result, I came up with a comprehensive list of indications and contra-indications for SST and published these in the first edition of my book, *Single-Session Integrated CBT (SSI-CBT): Distinctive Features* (Dryden, 2017). However, I soon realised several important things about these early endeavours.

First, I realised that I was bringing a conventional therapy mindset to the question of client suitability and unsuitability. Conventional therapists are quite concerned with the issue of who is and who is not suitable for their mode of therapy delivery and will devote much time to this in the client's first visit. Agencies based on this same mindset set out in their initial contact to determine who is suitable and unsuitable for the modes of therapy delivery that they offer. The IAPT service which did a pilot study on SST and have retained it have brought it into their normal practice of determining which form of therapy is suitable for which clients and have concluded that only clients with mild issues should be referred for SST. Clients' views are secondary to the agency's views on this matter.

Second, I saw that in developing this list of inclusion and exclusion criteria, I had to find of way of implementing it. It was when I concluded that the way I would have to do this was to devote my first contact with the person to assessing their suitability for SST rather than offering them therapy in that first contact that I realised the futility of what I was doing from what I call in this book, SST 'orientation' thinking.

Third, I was violating a major principle of SST – that it is client-led (see Chapter 8). By developing a list of inclusion and exclusion

DOI: 10.4324/9781032657752-7

criteria, I was, in effect, stating that I was the one determining whether a client should have SST or not rather than the client.

So, in writing the second edition of my book, *Single-Session Integrated CBT (SSI-CBT): Distinctive Features* (Dryden, 2022b), I omitted the chapter devoted to the 'suitability criteria' issue as I had quickly removed it from my practice of SST. In doing so, I updated the way I saw the issue and how I now view it from the SST 'orientation' thinking perspective.

My current view on the issue is summed up in the title of this chapter: potentially *anyone can* be helped in a session. However, this does not mean that *everyone will* be helped in a single session. Guidance on this point comes from the SST 'open-access, enter now' experience where anyone who arrives at such a facility is seen and helped to achieve their stated wants from the session. If they are in the wrong place or have goals that cannot be met, then they are given a respectful response and aided to find a more appropriate service to help them get what they want at that time.[1] It has often happened that people who could not be helped at their visit for whatever reason return later for help that can be dealt with in a single visit. Such people say that the reason they came back was that they were taken seriously when they came the first time and treated with respect. Even though they could not get what they wanted from their first visit, they returned because that visit was a positive experience for them.

It is perhaps easier to say who SST should not offered to: those who do not want it!

So the best answer to the question, *'Can a person be helped with SST?'* is to have a single session with them and at the end answer a different question, *'Has the person been helped with SST?'* This means offering everyone who wants it, a single session.

Let's pick up on the dialogue between an SST therapist and a conventional therapist on this point.

---

1 Such people may have been looking to change their medication which requires the aid of a physician, or they have been looking to be rehoused which does not come within the direct orbit of an 'open-access, enter now' centre. Such individuals are given a respectful hearing and referred to a more appropriate service.

Conventional therapist: You acknowledge that not everyone will be helped with SST although anyone can be helped. What attempts have been made to identify the kinds of people who don't benefit from SST?

SST therapist: Even if we could find a way of answering your question – which I don't believe we can for reasons I will make clear presently – I think that there is a danger in doing so.

For example, let's suppose we found that people with disorder 'x' tend not to be helped through SST – meaning that they do not find the first session helpful to them even though they have set a session goal that is potentially achievable. Don't forget that in SST more help is available, and it may be that at the end of the session the person themself and their therapist agree that the person will be better helped through ongoing work. If the agency offers such work, then the person can access it. If not, then a suitable referral is made to a different agency.

However, it is also possible that a given individual belonging to the same group will find SST helpful. That is why we take an individual-based approach to this issue and not a group-based approach. In other words, in answer to the question, 'Will Mary Smith be helped through SST that she has chosen to access?', we do the session and discover then if Mary found it helpful. We could spend her first visit trying to discover if she *may* find SST helpful and then offer her the session if the answer is 'yes', but instead we could offer the help that she has requested. Why hold up that process?

Also, let's suppose we do engage in the task of discovering which people may not benefit from SST. We will have to do a large-scale study and compare the people who have benefitted from SST with those who haven't. To do this, we will have to give everyone in that study a very large battery of tests since we don't know in advance which variables are likely to be key discriminators between the two groups. Let's suppose we do that. What will we find? My guess is that we will not find any key client variables that show who will and will not benefit from SST. My hunch is that the people who benefit from SST will be those who have a good alliance with their therapists and the people who do not benefit from SST will be those who have not formed a good alliance with their therapists. There is research with bears out my hunch (Simon, Imel, Ludman & Steinfeld, 2012).

Now, if my hunch is correct, then the question is not which clients can benefit from SST and which clients can't, but how can we find out in advance if a client and a therapist will form a good alliance in SST? The answer is that you can't do so with any degree of predictive validity. What you can do is to train therapists properly in SST so that they become adept at forming alliances with their clients quickly – a topic I will discuss more fully in Chapter 7.

Chapter 6

Focus on the Person, Not the Disorder

When I do training events on single-session therapy, one of the most frequently asked questions I get from the participants has a particular format, 'Does SST work with "x"' where "x" is a particular disorder or problem?' (see Dryden, 2022a). The disorders are usually indicative of some complexity such as a personality disorder, trauma or psychosis. I have a standard response to such questions which is, 'What is the person's name and what do they want to get from the session?' Note then that the question comes from someone holding a conventional therapy mindset and my response comes from the SST 'orientation' thinking part of the SST mindset.

People who ask the 'Does SST work with "x"?' type of questions tend to view the clinical world in terms of diagnoses and treatments for these diagnostic categories. From this perspective it makes no sense at all that a person with borderline personality disorder (BPD), for example, may be helped in one session or even a series of single sessions (as in 'One-At-A-Time' therapy). There are treatment protocols that last for many weeks if the person wants to engage fully in such treatment.[1] However, Mary who has a diagnosis of BPD is anxious about an upcoming interview and wants focused help with this issue. Should the SST therapist refuse to help her under these conditions because she has BPD? Our answer to this question is a decided, 'no' since she is clear about what she wants and wants imminent help. Assuredly, she would not be turned away if she came to an SST 'open-access, enter now' centre so why should she be denied single-session help because she has made an appointment for it? From

---

1 For example, DBT London offers modular-based treatment with support lasting 30 weeks. https://dbtlondon.com/ – accessed 21-04-23.

DOI: 10.4324/9781032657752-8

an SST 'orientation' thinking perspective she shouldn't. Now if Mary wants to address her BPD in one session in the sense that she wants to be free of it then, the SST therapist would be clear that they would not be able to do that. An important component of the SST 'orientation' thinking part of the SST mindset is that SST therapists are clear with themselves and with people seeking their help concerning what they can do and what they can't do.

Here is another example of where the focus was on the person and not on the disorder that I presented in Dryden (2023a):

> A person diagnosed with psychosis sought help from an 'open-access, enter now' clinic in a state of anxiety. What had been happening was that the client's landlord had found him agitated, talking to himself and was concerned that the client posed a risk to others in his building. He, thus, threatened the client with eviction. In the session, the therapist first responded by suggesting that the client might wish to review his medication with his psychiatrist, which he agreed to do. Then, as the client stated that his goal was to keep his accommodation, the therapist suggested that they role-played how the client could talk to his landlord to allay the latter's fears about the client posing a risk to the household. They did this, and the client implemented this solution with his landlord and successfully retained his accommodation. He was still diagnosed as psychotic, but he was psychotic and safe in his living quarters rather than psychotic and vulnerable living on the streets.

The SST therapist, therefore, has a very different perspective to a conventional therapist on this point. In SST, people are seen as unique individuals who may have problems that can be categorised in a number of different ways. We prefer to focus on the person and not the disorder. We won't ignore the disorder, but we recognise that if ten people who have been diagnosed with borderline personality disorder, for example, seek SST help, then they may all be seeking different things from the session, some the therapist may be able to help them with and some not. But to send away all ten people who have BPD because they have BPD is against the spirit of SST.

Let's pick up on the dialogue between an SST therapist and a conventional therapist on this point.

Conventional therapist: It seems to me if that if you begin therapy immediately with a person with a personality disorder, for example, then you may be opening up a can of worms that you won't be able to close by the end of the session and thus, you may end up by doing more harm than good.

SST therapist: I think your question is an important one and highlights the point that harm in therapy can happen in any form of therapy delivery. However, since you have focused on SST here let me respond in kind.

By 'opening up a can of worms' I assume you mean 'creating a complicated situation in which doing something to correct a problem leads to many more problems'. If so, the SST therapist would put in place a number of safeguards to minimise this happening.

First, the therapist would ask the client for a session goal and if this stated goal was unrealistic, they would explain the difficulties with such a goal and negotiate an achievable session goal.

Second, when therapist and client co-create a focus for the session and the therapist keeps checking in with the client that they are talking about what they want to talk about, then dealing with the issue that they client has nominated means that this would not lead to other problems coming up as they would do so if the 'can of worms' was opened.

Third, if the therapist was concerned about 'opening up a can of worms' they would be explicit about this and say something like, 'I'm concerned that we might discuss something that could be too painful for you to deal with today. Can I rely on you to tell me and if I notice that this might be happening, will you allow me to check this out with you?'

Fourth, there is the safeguard of further help being available at the end of the session. Thus, suppose that a client has begun to discuss something that might begin to open things up too much for them, the SST might intervene and say something like, 'Don't feel you have to go too deeply today, there is, don't forget, the prospect of more help being available for you after this session, if you want it'.

In general, when the client and therapist develop a good working alliance in the session (see the next chapter), then this is the best way of keeping any 'can of worms' firmly closed.

Complex Problems Do Not Require Complex Solutions

When a client has a complex problem that they wish to discuss in SST, the therapist will help them select a solution to their problem that they can implement and will make a difference to their life. This solution may not completely solve the client's problem but will help them to get unstuck so that they can take a few steps forward. The trouble with a complex solution is that it is difficult to remember and therefore difficult to implement even though it may be more effective than the simpler solution. A potent solution that is not implemented has no effect on the complex problem.

Chapter 7

The Client–Therapist Relationship Can Be Established Rapidly

As discussed in Chapter 5, there is evidence that those who benefit from a single session of therapy develop a good working alliance with their therapists and those who don't thus benefit do not develop such an alliance. It follows that a key ingredient in the effectiveness of SST (as well as, of course, in other forms of therapy delivery) is the quality of the working alliance that the therapist develops with their client.

One of the most common frequently asked questions about SST is, how can the therapist develop an effective working alliance with their client quickly when such an alliance takes a number of sessions to develop? (Dryden, 2022a).

The Four Domains of the Working Alliance

To answer the above question, it is useful first to consider the four major domains of the working alliance: bonds, views, goals and tasks (Bordin, 1979; Dryden, 2011).

Bonds

The *bond* between client and therapist refers to the quality of their interconnectedness. There are two components of this bond: the 'feeling' component and the 'working' component.

The Feeling Component

The feeling component of the bond in SST refers to the client's emotional experience of the therapist as the two work together. When the bond is strong for the client, they experience the therapist as empathic, respectful and genuine. Thus, the therapist's tasks are to demonstrate

DOI: 10.4324/9781032657752-9

that they understand the client's nominated issue from the client's perspective (empathy), indicate that the client's concerns are paramount in the session (respect) and be transparent about what SST is, and what they can and can't do in the session (genuineness).

The Working Component

The working component of the bond in SST is characterised by collaboration and negotiation. This is shown in the following ways:

- The client sets the direction and then collaborates with the therapist in taking this direction.
- There is explicit negotiation of problems and/goals.
- There is joint negotiation of a therapeutic focus.
- The two work together to find a solution.
- SST is a fusion between what the client brings to the process and what the therapist brings to the process.
- There is explicit negotiation about any further help that the client needs an agreed pathway for the client to use, if necessary.
- There is negotiation about follow-up – if it is to occur and if so, when?

Views

The domain of the working alliance that I have termed *views* refers to the various understandings that both client and therapist have about the process of SST. There are two components of these views: the practical and the therapeutic.[1]

The Therapeutic Component

The therapist and client need to have shared views about the following:

- What SST is.
- The therapist's or agency's confidentiality policy.

---

1 Here, I will only discuss the therapeutic component. The practical component refers to matters such as the therapist's or agency's cancellation policy and any fees due and how these are to be paid.

- What factors account for the client's nominated issue, and how they unwittingly maintain it.
- What constitutes effective therapy for this problem.
- What further help is available to the client and how they can access this help.

Goals

In the *goals* domain of the working alliance there are two goals that it is important that the therapist elicits from the client: a session goal and a problem-related goal.

Session Goal

As I discussed in Chapter 1, SST is purposive and its basic purpose is to help the client achieve their stated wants from the session. This is particularly important because the therapist does not know if they are going to see the person again. The alliance is strengthened when the therapist and client are united in helping the latter achieve their session goal. When a person is coming for help with a specific issue, then their session goal is often a solution to this problem.

Problem-Related Goal

If the client has come to SST for help with what I call a nominated problem or issue then it is useful for the client to assist the person to set a goal in relation to this problem. I call this the client's problem-related goal. The goal is the state reached by the client where they no longer have the problem. While it is not realistic for the client to achieve their problem-related goal by the end of the session, it is realistic for them to find a solution to this problem which they can implement after the session has ended and thus take steps to achieve their problem-related goal.

The Session Goal and Problem-Related Goal Are Related

As discussed above, when the person is seeking help for a problem from the SST therapist, this is frequently in the form of a solution which often constitutes their session goal. When implemented after the session, the solution helps the person to achieve their problem-session goal as defined above. This relationship is shown below. From an alliance perspective, what is important is that the therapist and client have a shared understanding of both goals and their relationship and that the therapist works with the client to achieve both.

Nominated ——————▶ **Solution** ——————▶ **Problem-Related Goal**
Problem   **Session Goal**   **(after the session)**

Tasks

In the *tasks* domain of the alliance, both the therapist and client have tasks to do to help the client to achieve their session and problem-related goals. From an alliance perspective, the therapist and client need to recognise their own tasks and those of the other and have a tacit agreement that they will carry out their own tasks.

The therapist's tasks will vary according to the help that the client is seeking (see Chapter 19). Thus, if the client wants to get things off their chest this calls for a different set of tasks than helping them to deal with a specific problem. Also, from an alliance perspective, it is important that the therapist offers tasks suited to the help the client requires.

Tasks Associated with Dealing with Emotional/ Behavioural Problems

In my experience the most frequently requested form of help from clients seeking SST is assistance with specific emotional/behavioural problems or issues. The therapist's tasks[2] associated with this helping stance involve them:

- Understanding the problem and how the client unwittingly maintains it.[3]
- Exploring solution possibilities.

---

2 All these are carried out with the client's full involvement.
3 Solution-focused SST therapists would not implement this task.

- Encouraging the client to choose the solution most likely to work from the client's perspective and in doing so, helping the client to use relevant internal and external resources.
- Suggesting that the client rehearses the solution to fine-tune it or select a better one.
- Helping the client to develop an action plan to implement the solution after the session.

Throughout this part of the SST process, the client's tasks involve them:

- Giving the therapist accurate responses to their questions.
- Orienting the therapist towards solutions that they are most likely to implement and away from solutions that won't work for them.
- Selecting a solution that they can integrate into their life.
- Engaging fully with the solution rehearsal process and feeding back what they learned from it.
- Engaging with the action-planning process and only agreeing with a plan to which they are prepared to commit.

Let's pick up on the dialogue between an SST therapist and a conventional therapist on this point.

Conventional therapist: I understand your points about developing a working alliance quickly, but there are many clients who need a lot more time to trust their therapist. How would you develop an alliance with such clients?

SST therapist: I would start with the assumption that since the person has chosen SST, then they are willing to see if they can benefit from it. I would not know at the outset if that person is going to need more time than the session that they are having to develop trust in me, so I would strive to form an alliance as quickly as possible with them. If, at the end of the session, we have not developed a sufficiently good alliance and the client wants more help, then they can have it as long as it is available to them. This may be ongoing therapy where they can take their time to develop trust in me or with another therapist if I am not available for ongoing work or the person wants to see someone else.

Chapter 8

SST Is Client-Led

A central feature of single-session therapy and one that the therapist keeps in mind as they come to practise SST is that the process is client-led. This means that the client is the best person to judge what is best for them concerning their mental health. Now, this does not mean that the therapist will go along with anything that the client wants and does not have a voice. Rather, it means that the therapist will voice any concerns about the direction the client wants to take if the therapist considers that this may be detrimental to the mental well-being of the client. This then leads to a discussion between the two with the purpose of finding a way forward that meets the needs oof the client and is not detrimental to their well-being.

This 'SST is client-led' principle is shown in the following ways which I will discuss in this chapter.

1 The client decides to access SST.
2 The client decides what they want to achieve from the session.
3 The client decides how much therapy they want.

The Client Decides to Access SST

When an agency delivers therapy services, it is common practice that this is done from a conventional therapy perspective. What will tend to happen is that when a person is referred to or refers themself to an agency, then the first substantial contact between the person and the agency is likely to involve assessment. The major purpose of this assessment is for the agency to determine a) whether it can help the person and, if so, b) which service it offers is best suited to the person's needs *as judged by the agency*. If the person has a part to play in this process, it is a minor one. This is precisely what happened

DOI: 10.4324/9781032657752-10

when SST was introduced into an IAPT agency (see Chapters 4 and 5). Clients were assessed for their suitability for SST rather than determining this for themselves.

For SST to be practised without the 'SST is client-led' principle being at the heart of the work, in my view, strips SST of a lot of its therapeutic potency. When this occurs what will happen is that only clients with minor issues (as judged by the agency) will be referred for SST. This is precisely what happened in the aforementioned IAPT agency.

So, if an agency is going to preserve the 'SST is client-led' principle while incorporating SST into their suite of therapy services, how can they do this? There are two ways of doing this: a) making the initial session a therapy session and see how things go; and b) giving the client information of all the services offered by the agency and having them select the service that best meets their needs from their perspective.

The 'Gateway' Approach

In an agency run on conventional therapy lines, the assessment session serves as the gateway into the agency and, as we have seen, at that meeting an agency representative basically decides on the therapy service best suited to the person. When the 'client leads' principle is woven into the fabric of the agency then the gateway into the service is one session of therapy to see if the therapist can help the person take away from the session what they have come for. If the person needs more help, they can have it. The only restriction here is if the agency does not offer the service that the client requests. When an SST gateway approach is used then about 50% of client are satisfied with what they got from the session and require no further help at that time (Young, 2018). If the client does not want to make use of the 'first session is a therapy session' approach, then they can opt to have an assessment session along more conventional therapy lines.

The Client Selects the Service

If an agency has decided to include SST as one of its modes of therapy delivery, then it needs to explain about this service and this explanation should stand alongside explanations of the other services that the agency offers. Then, if the agency is going to adopt a 'client leads' position, a client should be able to opt for the service that they think best meets their therapeutic need at that time. Thus, a client who opts for SST in an appointment-based agency is in the same position as a client who comes to an 'open-access, enter now' centre. In other words, their request will be met and if it turns out that they would be better suited to a different service than a suitable referral is made to that service at the end of the single session.

The Client Decides What They Want to Achieve from the Session

In single-session therapy, the client decides what they want to achieve from the session. Indeed, asking the client what they want to achieve from the session is one of the first questions that the SST therapist asks the client. They do so because the 'SST is client-led' principle is an important feature of what I am calling in this book, SST 'orientation' thinking.

The Structuring of Therapy in Conventional Therapy and in Single-Session Therapy

It should go without saying but when a client has a session of therapy, they should decide what they want to achieve from the session. However, often therapy is not structured like that. Thus, in conventional therapy, after an initial assessment to determine what is the best therapy for that person – which as I said above, the client has a voice, but not the dominant one – therapy is structured around a number of factors, two of which I discuss below. By contrast, single-session therapy is structured around what the client wants to focus on and on what they want to achieve from the session.

The Client's Diagnosis

In conventional therapy, after a diagnosis has been made, the most suitable therapy for that diagnosis is offered to the client and therapy proceeds according to 'therapy for someone who has that diagnosis'. For example, somebody who is diagnosed with social anxiety disorder will be offered an empirically supported treatment for that disorder which will last for a set number of sessions and may have a session-by-session protocol. This may make it difficult for the client to discuss an issue that lies outside of this therapy-by-disorder approach.

This approach to therapy is predicated on the idea that the person will complete their course of treatment. If they do not, then they are deemed to be a 'drop out' from treatment. In this approach, the client is generally *not* asked what they want to achieve by the end of any particular session as this has already been determined by the therapist implementing the selected treatment programme.

By contrast, in SST the client's diagnosis holds little interest for the therapist since the session is not based on the client's diagnosis. Thus, ten people with diagnosis 'x' may want ten different things from the session.

The Client's Therapy Goals

In the conventional way of doing therapy, what the client wants to achieve by the end of therapy is discussed early on in the process and serves as a beacon for the process of therapy. These goals may change over the course of therapy so that therapist and client need to review the latter's therapy goals routinely and readjust their therapeutic approach accordingly.

This approach to therapy is again based on the assumption that the client will stay in therapy long enough to achieve their therapy goals or feel sufficiently confident that they can achieve these goals on their own having derived much benefit from the therapy sessions they have had. The number of sessions the client has is determined by the client's therapy goals.

Again, the client is generally not asked for their session goals as the focus is on the end of therapy and not the end of any particular session.

As we have seen, eliciting the client's session goal and helping the person to work towards them is a prime feature of SST.

The Client Decides How Much Therapy They Want and What Service They Wish to Access

In SST, the therapist recognises that, in effect, the client decides how many sessions to have and often opts to have one session. This is shown by the modal data that I discussed in Chapter 2. As Hoyt, Young and Rycroft (2020: 224) say, 'clients are far less interested in psychotherapy than are therapists and prefer brief therapeutic encounters.' While there are, of course, exceptions to this statement, it does tally with the modal data.

This principle is also evident at the end of the session when the therapist and client discuss what help the client wants to access, if any, and how they want to access it.[1] We know that in a 'gateway' service where all clients are offered a therapy session on their first visit rather than an assessment session, that 50% are satisfied with that one session and do not request further help at that time. With the other 50%, the client and therapist discuss the available options and the client is given up-to-date information concerning the wait times for these available services. Based on this information, the client may choose to wait until they have implemented what they have learned from the single session to decide what to do, or they may nominate a particular service that they want to access. Whatever, they decide, they will receive the help of their choosing unless the therapist has a good reason to show their concern about this choice as discussed at the beginning of this chapter.

Let's pick up on the dialogue between an SST therapist and a conventional therapist on this point.

Conventional therapist: Your point about SST being client-led may be laudable, but it implies that the client knows more about mental health issues than the therapist. Surely, the therapist is the expert on such matters and should be able to bring their expertise to help the client in ways that the client has not thought about?

SST therapist: You raise a very delicate issue. In SST, what we want to avoid is someone other than the client determining what is best for the person. Our point is that is the client's life and they should be able to determine how much or how little help they want from a therapist or from an agency. Conventional therapy is based on the assumption that all clients should be offered the

---

1 There are different viewpoints in the SST community on this point. Some think that deciding upon accessing further help should be done by clients at the end of the single session. Others think that clients should be invited to make such a decision after they have had an opportunity to reflect on their learning, digest it and then act on it.

best possible help according to the therapist's or agency's determination of their problems. However, as we have seen from the modal visit data, many clients do not behave according to conventional therapy's ideal. As I have discussed, clients will choose the number of sessions they want to attend, and this is often far less than this ideal.

That being said, there is nothing to prevent the therapist offering an informed opinion as long as this is in the service of what the client is looking for. There may also be times when the client may not see what is possible and the therapist may point this out, but this should be done tentatively and not from an 'I know best because I am the expert' position. However, the client should be free to reject the client's suggestions and it is important that the therapist creates a therapeutic climate where the client feels free to do this.

The therapist's skill in SST may be based, in part, on what they know but it is more founded on being flexible enough to offer the client what they want from therapy. This may mean, of course, that some may want longer therapeutic help with problems recognised according to standard diagnostic categories. However, many clients want a bit of help and when they receive this, they can get on with living their life, which has been enhanced by what they have taken away from the session.

Chapter 9

The Power of Now

Introduction

In his famous book, *The Power of Now*, Eckhart Tolle (1999) makes the point that 'now' is the only time that truly exists. This principle is part of SST 'orientation' thinking in that when the therapist thinks about doing the work, they do not know whether or not they will see a particular client again. As a result, when they conduct the session, they proceed on the basis that they won't see the person again, but are open to the possibility that they may.

Conventional therapy is based on what may be called 'The Power of the Future'. As we have seen, many therapy agencies offer a new client an assessment interview at their first point of substantial contact. This practice is based on two assumptions: i) the client will return after the first session and ii) the client will stay the course of their allocated treatment. And yet, again, as we have seen, many clients do not behave according to either of these assumptions. As Talmon (1990) discovered when he found that many of his clients would only attend for one session when he expected them to attend for more, the response of his colleagues was to bemoan the fact that the client population[1] was difficult to engage and not very psychologically minded. To the contrary, Talmon found that many of these clients had got what they had come for and did not require further help at that time. Talmon's response to this was to take action. Joining forces with his colleagues, Michael Hoyt and Robert Rosenbaum, they developed a mode of therapy delivery known as 'Planned Single-Session Therapy' and invited clients to engage with this service. What they found was

---

1 Talmon worked at that time at the Kaiser Permanente clinic in Hayward, North California.

DOI: 10.4324/9781032657752-11

that virtually all clients accepted this invitation to take part in this new way of working with the exception of one group – clients who were therapists themselves! Nothing much has changed over the years and therapists remain sceptical about SST and find it difficult to act according to the 'power of now' principle.

'The Power of Now' Exercise

There are two parts to this exercise.

Part 1

Imagine that a client has been referred to you for a block of six sessions in an agency where you work. When the client comes for their first session, it is with the expectation that you will see them for five additional sessions. Answer the following questions relating to this situation:

- What do you do to introduce the work and build rapport?
- What questions would you ask in the session?
- How would you decide what to focus on?
- How would you bring the session to a close?
- What feedback would you share with the client before rebooking for the second of six sessions?

Part 2

The morning before you conduct the session, the client informs you that they are unexpectedly going away on business for a year the day following your session, but they still want to have the session with you. They do not want online sessions while they are away. Would you still see them, knowing that you would probably not see them again?

If you would see them under these changed circumstances, answer the following questions:

- What do you do to introduce the work and build rapport?
- What questions would you ask in the session?
- How would you decide what to focus on?
- How would you bring the session to a close?

- What feedback would you share with the client before wishing them well?
- If you would not see them under these changed circumstances, why not?

Reflections

If you answered these two sets of questions differently, you might find it useful to ask yourself what led you to do so. As you consider this, ask yourself one further question. Assume now that you have had the first session with the client and that person does not go away the following day. How do you know for certain that you will see the person again? I hope you can see that you don't know whether you will or not. All you know is that you are seeing them in your office or online space during that first session. Given that you don't know whether or not you will see the client again, does this change the way you run the first session?[2]

If you gave the same answers to both sets of questions, then you are already engaged in SST 'orientation' thinking.

Let's pick up on the dialogue between an SST therapist and a conventional therapist on this point.

Conventional therapist: Your point that a therapist does not know for certain that a client will return for a second session is factually the case, but there are many situations in life where this is the case, Thus, I don't know if I will see my family this evening since I don't know for certain that I will get home safely. However, I make the assumption that I will. What is so wrong with a therapist assuming that a client will return for a second session and run the first session based on that assumption?

Single-session therapist: In SST, the reason why we conduct the session as if we won't see the person again (while accepting the possibility that we may) is that there is about a 40% chance that the client won't attend the second session, particularly in

---

2 Remember that in the second part of the exercise above, you know for certain that you will not see the person again.

an agency where SST is offered. You know that there is a very high chance of you getting home safely since you have had that experience many times. So, in both situations, the person concerned is guided by experience.

There is more to lose when a therapist holds back on offering the client therapy in the first session and that person does not come back, than there is when the therapist offers the client therapy in that session and then the client does not return. The client is more likely to benefit from the session in the second scenario than in the first.

Chapter 10

Less Is More

When my dear mother was alive and I visited her, she would not be happy unless she had fed me well and unless I took away a great deal of food 'for later'. My mother operated on the position that 'more is more'. Since love is expressed through food, the more she gave me to eat, then and later, the more love she had for me. While this may work for Jewish mothers and their sons, it does not work in single-session therapy.

Therapists new to SST also operate according to this 'more is more' position. They think that as they may only see the person once then they are obligated to encourage the client to take away as much they can from the session, otherwise they will consider that they have short-changed the client. The therapist who operates on this 'more is more' position will tend to cram too much into the session or send the client a lot of material after the session has ended to ensure that they have covered all the bases with a client. Some clients of these therapists have reported feeling quite overwhelmed by the SST experience and have ended up by taking away very little or nothing from it.

These therapists need to learn that 'less is more' and that if a client is to be helped to benefit from SST particularly when they want help with a specific emotional or behavioural problem in which they are stuck, they are best helped by taking away one or two points that they can implement after the session. SST therapists who adhere to the 'less is more' principle guard against any tendency they experience to give the client more particularly towards the end of the session when they have quite a bit of time left. This is why it is best to end the session when the work has been done even if this occurs before

DOI: 10.4324/9781032657752-12

50 minutes[1] has elapsed. If SST is conducted 'by the clock', and the therapist and client have finished their work after 35 minutes, for example, then the therapist will invite the client to discuss something else and, in my opinion, the new work will dilute the experience of what has gone before, and the client will take away less after 50 minutes than they would have done after 35 minutes. This again shows the value of the 'less is more' principle in SST.

Let's pick up on the dialogue between an SST therapist and a conventional therapist on this point.

Conventional therapist: While there may be clients who can only take away one or two points, aren't there also clients who can potentially take away more from the experience? Aren't you short-changing this latter group by restricting them to one or two points?

Single-session therapist: Yes, there may be clients who can take away more from the session than one or two points, but we have no way of knowing in advance who they are. In this sense, we prefer to play safe and not take a gamble that a given client can take away more from the experience. With these clients we argue that they can take away more from the experience by reflecting on how they can generalise their learning from the session to other areas of their life. In this respect, the 'more' that you mention concerns *breadth* of learning rather than *amount* of learning.

---

1 I am often asked how long a single session should last for. I am aware that this ranges from 30 minutes to 90 minutes. The length of the session will depend, in part, on how much mandatory areas the client has to cover. For example, in some agencies, therapists are mandated to cover certain ground and carry out a risk assessment with all clients. In these circumstances the single session will last longer than when conducted by therapists who are not mandated in this regard to do carry out such tasks. Here, I am using 50 minutes because in my view, in most circumstances this is enough time to do the work.

Chapter 11

Take Nothing for Granted

The last principle that forms a part of what I have called SST 'orientation' thinking is 'take nothing for granted'. We have seen how this principle led, in part, to the development of modern-day, single-session therapy as marked by the publication of Moshe Talmon's (1990) book, *Single Session Therapy: Maximizing the Effect of the First (and Often Only) Therapeutic Encounter*. Moshe began his work at the Kaiser Permanente clinic in North California by taking for granted that if clients signed up for therapy over time, then they would turn up for these sessions. He was wrong; two hundred only turned up for one session. When discussing this phenomenon with his colleagues they also had experienced this, but attributed this to the lack of psychological mindedness of the clinic's clientele. This time, Talmon did not take this explanation for granted. He contacted these two hundred patients and discovered that over 70% were pleased with the session and required no further assistance at that time.

In conventional therapy, it is taken for granted that if a person only attends for one session of therapy, they did not find the session helpful. To describe this, we say things like they have 'dropped out' of treatment or terminated therapy 'prematurely'. However, as we have seen, more often than expected people find the first session helpful and decide that they require no further assistance. They can be said to have ended therapy 'maturely'.

In truth, when somebody chooses not to return after a first session, we cannot take it for granted that they have or have not found the session helpful. We need to discover this from the person themself after the session.

In addition, it sometimes happens that a single-session therapist thinks that the session they have just had with a client was very productive with the client fully engaged in the session. The therapist

DOI: 10.4324/9781032657752-13

predicts that the client found it beneficial, but when the client feeds back it is to say that they were disappointed with the session and got little from it. Conversely, it also happens that an SST therapist thinks that a session with a client was unproductive. There was no focus and the client moved from topic to topic despite the best efforts of the therapist to keep the client on track. The therapist predicts that the client did not find the session beneficial, but when the client feeds back it is to say that they were very happy with the session and got a lot from it.

As we say in single-session therapy, take nothing for granted.

Part II

SST 'Pre-Session' Thinking

By SST 'pre-session' thinking, I refer to the thinking that the SST therapist engages in while actively preparing to do SST. In dealing with this part of the mindset, I will discuss the following:

- informing clients about SST;
- responding to potential clients when they ask questions about SST;
- eliciting informed consent from clients;
- helping clients to prepare for the session; and
- preparing oneself mentally for the session.

DOI: 10.4324/9781032657752-14

Chapter 12

Informing Potential Clients about SST

Once a therapist or agency has decided to offer single-session therapy then they need to think about how to inform potential clients about SST. I will concentrate here on the content of such information. How they communicate this information will be through websites and leaflets to potential clients and to potential referrers.

Disseminating ONEplus¹ Therapy in Independent Practice through a Website

On my website, the following information appears about ONEplus therapy:

What Is ONEplus Therapy?

ONEplus therapy occurs when you and I agree to meet for one session with the intention of me helping you to walk away from the session with the help you are looking for, which, when you implement it, will make a meaningful difference to your life. It is also important for you to realise that more help is available should you request it.

[The other services that I offer are also on my website.]

Is ONEplus Therapy for Me?

ONEplus therapy is for you if you are stuck with an emotional or behavioural problem and are looking for a way to get

---

1 See Chapter 1 for an explanation of why I refer to my SST work as ONEplus therapy.

DOI: 10.4324/9781032657752-15

unstuck. It is not for you if you seek ongoing therapy to address your problems.

[I am aware that different clients may want different forms of help from SST and I discuss these in Chapter 19. However, in my independent practice I wanted to specialise in offering single-session help for people feeling stuck with an emotional or behavioural problem.]

For Which Issues Can ONEplus Therapy Be Helpful?

ONEplus therapy can help you address the same issues that can be addressed in other forms of therapy delivery. The difference is that in ONEplus therapy, we will work from moment one to help you to take away what you have come for on the issue you have chosen to discuss with me. Thus, in ONEplus therapy, I do not take a case history or carry out an extensive assessment of you and your problems.

Can I Prepare for ONEplus Therapy?

Once you decide to have ONEplus therapy, I will send you a contract to sign. On receipt, we will make an appointment. Beforehand, I will send you a pre-session questionnaire to complete and return. While this is optional, the questionnaire is designed to help you prepare for the session so that you get the most from it. Sharing your questionnaire with me before the session also helps me prepare for the session.

[Before the Covid-19 pandemic I used to do pre-session telephone calls designed to help the client prepare for the session which was, in those days, face-to-face. The pandemic meant that most counselling services were offered online. As a result I offered SST by Zoom and to distinguish the session from the pre-session preparation for the session, I devised a pre-session questionnaire for clients to complete and return.

The main difference between the client completing the pre-session questionnaire and engaging in a pre-session telephone call with me (apart from cost) was that in about 20% cases the pre-session telephone preparation session was sufficient for the client and they did not need the face-to-face session whereas this has never happened with the pre-session questionnaire.]

What Does ONEplus Therapy Involve?

At the beginning of the session, I will check that you understand the purpose of the session, and if so, I will help you to clarify what you want to take away from the session. We will then agree on a focus for the session, which is usually the issue for which you seek help. It is my responsibility to help us both keep to this focus. I will then help you to discover a potential solution to the problem and encourage you to rehearse it in the session to see if it is right for you. If so, I will help you develop a plan to implement the solution and clarify your takeaways from the session.

What Happens at the End of the Session?

At the end of the session, we will discuss the next steps.[2] The options are i) You conclude that you got what you came for and need no further help; ii) You indicate that you would like some time to reflect on the session, put into practice what you learned and then decide if you need further help and iii) You decide that you would like further help which might include having another session, having an agreed block of sessions or opting for ongoing therapy. If, at the end of the session, we agree that you need more specialised help than I can provide, then I will help you find such help.

Is There Anything Else I Need to Know?

- At the moment, I am only offering ONEplus therapy online.
- With your permission, I will record the session and send you an audio recording of the session free of charge.
- If you want a written transcript, I can provide one at what it costs me to have it transcribed professionally.

---

2 See note 1 on page 42.

Disseminating ONEplus Therapy in Independent Practice through a Leaflet

Not all therapists have a website, and not all clients consult therapists' websites for information about their services. Consequently, an SST in independent practice may wish to prepare a leaflet on SST therapy for potential clients. This can be sent to those enquiring about SST and it can also be put on noticeboards of relevant places such as GP surgeries.

Below I provide an example of a leaflet that I devised explaining ONEplus therapy which I send out to potential clients interested in learning more about this form of therapy delivery.

What Is ONEplus Therapy

Information for Prospective Clients

Windy Dryden

- ONEplus Therapy is an intentional endeavour where you and I set out with the purpose of helping you in one session, on the understanding that more help is available to you if you want it.
- At the end of the session, we will agree on a way forward.[3] Thus, i) you may decide to seek no further help; ii) you may decide to reflect on and digest what you learned in the session, act on what you learned and see what happens before deciding whether to seek further help; or iii) you may decide to arrange for further help at the end of the session. If the latter, we can discuss what further help is available so you can choose what best suits you. Each of these ways forward is equally OK.
- ONEplus Therapy is based on offering help at the point of need rather than at the point of availability. It has the effect of you being seen quickly when you need help.
- ONEplus Therapy is based on three foundations:

  - The most frequent number of sessions clients have internationally is '1', followed by '2', '3', and so on
  - 70–80% of those who have one session are satisfied with that session, given their current circumstances

---

3 See note 1 on page 42.

- Therapists are poor at predicting who will attend only one session and who will attend more.

[Given that this leaflet may be seen in places such as GP surgeries by people who know nothing about ONEplus therapy/ SST, I make the case for this mode of therapy delivery here.]

- My primary goal in ONEplus Therapy is to provide you with help to address a specific issue with which you are stuck. Here I will help you to take a few steps forward, which may encourage you to travel the rest of the journey without my professional assistance.

[Again, while I am aware that some people may want other things from ONEplus therapy/SST, in my independent practise I specialise in helping those who seek help for a specific issue with which they are stuck.]

- People have found it helpful to prepare for the session so that they can get the most from it. To this end, I will send you a questionnaire to complete and return. This is NOT compulsory, but it helps us both prepare for the session.
- The focus of a session in ONEplus Therapy is on us negotiating a goal for that session. If you have a specific issue that you wish to address, I will help you to find and rehearse a solution that facilitates the achievement of this goal. Then, I will help you to devise an action plan which you can implement after the session.
- In ONEplus Therapy, I will help you to:

  - Discover what you have done in the past to deal with your problem. I will then encourage you to use what has been helpful and set aside what has not been helpful.
  - Identify and use your internal strengths and external resources in implementing the agreed solution.

- I encourage follow-up to discover how you are getting on and to improve service delivery, and at the end of the session, we will make an appointment for a follow-up, but only if you wish.

Chapter 13

Responding to Potential Clients' Questions about SST

Even though therapists and agencies will make information available to potential clients through websites and leaflets as we have seen in the previous chapter, a particular person may have questions about SST which they will approach the agency or independent practitioner for answers. Most often these questions will be asked through email or by phone. In my view, since one of SST's key principles involves responding speedily to people's requests for help, the therapist or agency representative needs also to respond speedily to answer their questions or requests for information. In what follows, I will draw on my own experiences.

Potential Clients' FAQs

If I am contacted by someone asking about SST and they have not looked at my website or read the leaflet I have prepared, I will encourage them to do the former or will offer to send the latter by email attachment. I do this because I do not want to provide information that is readily available. Once the person has consulted the relevant section on ONEplus therapy[1] or read the leaflet that I have sent them, I am happy to answer their questions. Here is a sample of ten questions that potential clients ask me together with my responses.

1 *Will you only see me once?*

No. While my main objective in ONEplus therapy is to work with you to help you achieve what you have come for from the session,

---

1 Remember that I refer to my SST work as ONEplus therapy.

DOI: 10.4324/9781032657752-16

further help is available, usually after a period where you reflect on, digest and act on your learning from the session. That is why the word 'plus' is featured in the title of my approach to this work. It is more traditionally known as 'single-session therapy', but I use the term ONEplus therapy because it is easy to think that single-session therapy means a therapy that lasts for a single session. It doesn't mean that, but the name leads people to come to that conclusion.

2   *What can I realistically expect to achieve in one session?*

It depends on what you are struggling with and what you want to achieve from the session. As I don't know anything about you, let me answer your question more generally. I strive to help people who are stuck with an emotional or a behavioural problem, find a way to get unstuck, a way that they can implement after the session has finished and see what happens as a result. If a person needs more help after a period of implementation, then that is available. So, I see what you can realistically achieve as the beginning of a process not the end of the problem. Having said that, occasionally it does happen that the person resolves their problem in one visit. When this happens, it does so because the person has put the issue that they have been struggling with into a new frame. When a problem is habitual, however, it takes longer to deal with.

3   *How do I know if I will benefit from ONEplus therapy?*

When I began doing what I call ONEplus therapy, I drew up a list of indications and contraindications to help me to answer the very question you have just asked. However, I quickly discovered that I was barking up the wrong tree. What I was doing was developing a single assessment session to see who might benefit from a single therapy session. What I do now is to say honestly that the only way we will both discover if you will benefit from ONEplus therapy is for us to have the session and answer the question at the end of the session rather than before the session has begun.

From my work as a practitioner doing ONEplus therapy in a number of settings, my experience is that clients are more likely to benefit from ONEplus therapy if they want to access this way of working, they have realistic expectations of what they can achieve from it, they are open to consider different potential solutions to their problem, they work with me as an active collaborator and they are prepared to implement what they have learned from the session.

I am not saying that people who lack one or more of these factors won't benefit from ONEplus therapy. What I am saying is that the more these factors are present, the more likely it is that the person will benefit.

4   *How does ONEplus therapy work?*

My approach to ONEplus therapy is as follows. Once we have contracted to work with one another, I send you a pre-session questionnaire for you to complete, the main purpose of which is to help you to prepare for the session so that you get the most from it. I invite you to send me a copy of your completed questionnaire to help me to prepare for the session as well. Then when we meet (either face-to-face or by Zoom), I will begin by asking you to confirm the issue that you want to deal with in the session. I will ask you what you want to achieve by the end of the session from discussing the issue with me. Having agreed this as a focus, it is my job to help us both stay on track. I will help us both understand the issue you are bringing up and why you are stuck with it. I will help you to find a solution to the problem so that you can get unstuck from it. Once we have found a solution, I will suggest that you rehearse it in the session so that you can confirm that it suits you and is likely to be helpful to you. If so, I will encourage you to make a plan to implement the solution after we finish. If you wish, we will have a follow-up to see how you are getting on. You can access further help at any time.

5   *I have 'x' disorder. Can you help me with ONEplus therapy?*

It depends on what you want to achieve by the end of the session. If, for example, you want your disorder to be gone, then I doubt very much that I can help you to do that. If however, you are looking for a way to address an issue (that may be related or unrelated to your disorder) that you can implement after the session then that is doable.

6   *Is there a risk with ONEplus therapy?*

There is a risk with all modes of therapy delivery. In my view, the risks associated with ONEplus therapy are minimised for the following reasons: i) we will be working towards a goal for the session that you have chosen; ii) you are in charge of what you want to discuss. I will not push you to discuss matters that you do not want to discuss; iii) we will be working together as a team to your selected agenda. We will not be working to my agenda. Indeed, if I have an agenda, it is to work to your agenda; iv) if you have not found the session valuable, you have made no commitment to return.

7   *Isn't ONEplus therapy a bit of a rush?*

It may seem like that, but my experience is that when practised well, ONEplus therapy unfolds in a relaxed, but focused manner.

8   *What is the purpose of the recording of the session and the transcript?*

Whenever, I conduct a ONEplus therapy session in my independent practice, I record the session for the client's later review. This is included in the price for the session. If the client also wants the written transcript for later review, I send it to a professional transcriber that I use and charge the client what the transcriber charges me. Some clients prefer the audio recording, some the transcript and some benefit from both.

9   *Do many therapists practise ONEplus therapy?*

ONEplus therapy is the name that I have given to my work in the field which is generally known as single-session therapy. As such, only I practise ONEplus therapy. However, if we change your question to, 'Do many therapists practise single-session therapy?' the answer is not many in the UK, but the numbers are growing. I have devoted the latter part of my career to disseminating SST and training therapists in it in the UK. Internationally, SST is practised in the USA, Canada, Australia, Italy, Sweden and elsewhere.

10 *A lot of my friends are therapists and counsellors and they all dismiss what you call ONEplus therapy or single-session therapy as foolish and impractical. What makes you right and them wrong?*

For me it is not a matter of right and wrong. You do not say how much your therapist and counsellor friends know about ONEplus therapy or single-session therapy, but I suspect not a lot. Also, my guess is that their judgments stem from what I call a conventional therapy mindset where therapy begins with an assessment and unfolds over time based on that initial assessment. From this perspective, I can understand why ONEplus therapy or SST seems foolish and practical. However, if they viewed this mode of therapy delivery from a ONEplus therapy or single-session therapy mindset, I think that they would come to a different conclusion.

Chapter 14

Eliciting Informed Consent from Clients

Informed consent is a central ethical principle in all forms of therapy delivery. Eliciting informed consent from clients in single-session therapy involves, as the term makes clear, two components:

1 An *informing* component where the therapist gives the prospective client enough information about single-session therapy and what it involves and about other salient aspects of the therapy process that allows the client to make an informed decision about whether or not to participate in single-session therapy. Part of this process involves the prospective client asking the therapist questions, the answers to which have a bearing on whether they choose to give their informed consent to proceed.
2 A *consenting* component where the prospective client, based on the information provided to them by the therapist and on the answers to their questions, gives their verbal or written consent to participate in single-session therapy. At this point, they become a client.

Barnett (2015) outlines a number of benefits of informed consent that are in accord with a number of elements of SST 'orientation' thinking (see also Snyder & Barnett, 2006):

- It promotes client autonomy.
- It helps to foster the collaborative bond between the therapist and client.
- It strengthens other aspects of the working alliance between the therapist and client particularly in the *views* domain of the alliance (see Chapter 7).

DOI: 10.4324/9781032657752-17

What Should Be Covered in the Informed Consent Process

While different therapists and agencies will have their own views on this issue, drawing on Barnett (2015), my standpoint is that the following information should be given to prospective SST clients:

- The nature and anticipated course of SST.
- The psychotherapist's credentials and relevant professional experience in SST.
- The fact that the client's participation in SST is voluntary and they have a right not to engage in SST despite the stance of other stakeholders.
- What other therapy options are available to them and the amount of time they have to wait to access these options.
- The therapist's or agency's fee and payment policy and the associated cancellation policy.
- Confidentiality and its limits to include all applicable mandatory reporting requirements.
- The involvement of any third parties.
- Any potential risks.

Informed Consent: Verbal or Written?

Therapists and agencies differ on whether they seek verbal or written consent from prospective SST clients. My own position is that since one of the principles that underlies the ethical practice of SST is 'clarity', I ask my clients to sign and date a contract that I use which signifies to all concerned that the person has given their informed consent to proceed. At that point they become a client (Seabury, Seabury & Garvin, 2011). I have included my ONEplus therapy contract in Appendix 1.

When to Elicit Informed Consent?

Obviously, the SST therapist needs to elicit informed consent from the client before the session begins. Otherwise, therapy would have started before such consent has been given.

In my own independent practice, the process is usually as follows. Once I have answered any questions a prospective client may have about SST, and they indicate that they wish to proceed to access this form of therapy delivery, I will send them my therapy contract (see Appendix 1) along with my explanatory leaflet on ONEplus therapy. If I have already sent them the leaflet beforehand, I will just send them the contract.

In the contract, I say the following, 'If you have any questions about ONEplus therapy or the terms of this contract that you want answered before you give your informed consent to proceed, please email them to me. Only sign the contract when your questions have been answered to your satisfaction'.

If you are thinking about offering SST in your independent practice or if the agency in which you work is thinking about doing so, then you need to give some thought about when to deal with the issue of informed consent and when to ask the client to give informed consent to proceed.

I will also cover eliciting informed consent in Chapter 17 when I deal with how to begin an SST session.

Chapter 15

Helping Clients to Prepare for the Session

In single-session therapy by appointment, once the client has given their informed consent to proceed with SST and after they have made an appointment to have the session, then the therapist should email the client to introduce themself, if necessary, and to invite the client to complete a pre-session questionnaire.[1] The thinking behind this part of the SST process is twofold. First, SST is very time efficient. If there is time between the SST appointment being made and that appointment taking place, then it is important that the client be encouraged to make good use of it. Second, if the client prepares I for the session, then they will get more from it than if they are not prepared. The purpose of the pre-session questionnaire, therefore, is to encourage the client to make such preparations.

This is also the case in an 'open-access, enter now' SST centre because it is likely that a person coming into such a centre will have to wait for a short period of time and in this instance, they can be asked to make the best use of this waiting time by completing a pre-session questionnaire.

In both scenarios, once the client has completed the questionnaire, they are invited to return a copy to the therapist so that the latter can find out a little about how the client wants to use the session and what they want to achieve from it.

---

1 It is important to make clear to the client that the completion of the pre-session questionnaire is voluntary.

DOI: 10.4324/9781032657752-18

An Example of a Pre-Session Questionnaire

In what follows, I present and discuss a pre-session questionnaire that I use in my ONEplus therapy work. I do not suggest that this is *the* way of devising such a form, but *a* way of so doing.

Pre-Session Questionnaire

I have found it helpful to ask clients to prepare for their session with me, and to that effect, I would be grateful if you would complete this form. Let me emphasise that this is not mandatory; just something that will help you get the most from our session. If you decide to complete it, I would be grateful if you would share a copy with me by email attachment so I can prepare for our session too.

[People are used to being asked to complete forms from organisations that appear to benefit the organisations rather than themselves. Thus, I found it important to state that the main purpose for the client to complete this form is for their benefit: to help them prepare for the session so that they get the most from it. I also want to stress the principle of client determination here by emphasising that the completion of the form is voluntary. Finally, I emphasise the collaborative nature of ONEplus therapy (SST) by stating that I would appreciate receiving a copy of the client's completed form so that I can prepare for the session as well.]

Name: **Date:**

1   What is the issue that you want to focus on in the session?

Be concise. In one or two sentences get to the heart of the problem, if possible.

[The ONEplus therapy service that I run in my independent practice is primarily for people who want to deal with a specific issue with which they are stuck. There are other forms of help available in SST which I will discuss in Chapter 19. In most approaches to SST, focus is vital and note that I have stressed this twice in the above rubric: i) by inviting the person to select an issue which will be the focus of our session; ii) by inviting them to be concise in their description of the issue and to get to the 'heart of the problem'.]

2   Why is this significant?

What's at stake? How does this affect your life? What is the future impact if the issue is not resolved?

[blank box]

[In this question, I want the client to be clear with themself and with me about why it is important for them to address their nominated[2] issue with me.]

3   What is your goal in discussing this issue in the session?

What are the specific results you would like to achieve by the end of the session that would give you the sense that you have begun to make progress on the issue?

[blank box]

---

2 In this book, I refer to the issue or problem that the client chooses to address with me as their 'nominated' issue/problem.

[While all therapy is goal-directed (Mahrer, 1967; Cooper & Law, 2018), in ONEplus therapy (SST) we focus on the client's goals for the session. This flows from the first feature of SST 'orientation' thinking that I discussed in Chapter 1: that we join with the client to help them achieve what they have come for from the session and ensure that further help is available to them on request. At the outset, however, we do not know if a specific client will be satisfied with a single session or will require more. To give them the best chance of achieving what they want from the session, we ask them for their session goal and help them work towards this in a focused way.]

4   Specify briefly the relevant background information.

What you think I need to know about the issue to help you with it? Summarise in bullet points.

```
┌────────────────────────────────────────────────┐
│                                                │
│                                                │
│                                                │
│                                                │
│                                                │
└────────────────────────────────────────────────┘
```

[During the session I find it useful to place in context the issue the person has nominated for change. I am also interested in what the client thinks it is important for me to know about the issue.]

5   How have you tried to deal with the issue up to this point?

What steps, successful or unsuccessful have you taken so far in addressing the issue?

```
┌────────────────────────────────────────────────┐
│                                                │
│                                                │
│                                                │
│                                                │
│                                                │
└────────────────────────────────────────────────┘
```

[When people seek help because they have an emotional or behavioural problem with which they are stuck, they have usually made a number of attempts to solve this problem themselves. They may also have sought help from others, both lay and professional. It is important for SST therapists to find about these attempts in order to build upon what has gone before. In particular, in the session the SST therapist can capitalise on the client's helpful attempts[3] to deal with the problem and to distance themself from the client's unhelpful attempts.]

6   What are the strengths or inner resources that you have as a person that you could draw upon while tackling the issue?

If you struggle with answering this question, think of what people who really know you and who are on your side would say.

[The SST therapist builds on what is within the client themself and in the client's environment in order to help the person to achieve their session goals. This question and the following one encourage the client to think about this issue in advance so that they can draw upon these factors as they work with the therapist to get the most from the session.]

3   Even though the client still has the problem they may have found that certain attempts to help themselves or be helped by others to have been partially successful and if so, their therapist can encourage them to build on this in the session.

7 Who are the people in your life who can support you as you tackle
   the issue?

   Name them and say what help each can provide.

Windy Dryden

Chapter 16

Preparing Oneself for the Session

When a therapist who has initially been trained in the mindset and practice of conventional therapy is subsequently trained in the mindset and practice of single-session therapy, that person generally needs a period to adjust to this change of mindset and practice. This is complicated by the fact that such therapists will at the same time probably also continue to practice conventional therapy.

How to Facilitate Adjustment to SST

However, there are a number of things that a therapist can do to facilitate their adjustment to SST. These are:

- having supervision;
- developing peer support; and
- being mindful of one's vulnerabilities as an SST therapist before the session.

Supervision

Once a therapist has been trained in single-session therapy and has started to do SST work it is vital that they have this work supervised by a person experienced in doing SST and in supervising SST therapists. Different forms of supervision offer the therapist different things.

Case Discussion

In case discussion, the therapist discusses their SST work with their supervision and other group members (if the supervision is taking

DOI: 10.4324/9781032657752-19

place in a group). From the perspective of helping the therapist to adjust to SST work, the supervisor needs to create an atmosphere where the therapist can discuss their difficulties with both the SST mindset itself, and with implementing SST.

Therapist: I started off the session well and was able to elicit the client's problem and session goal and helped the client to stay focused. However, when the client mentioned, in passing, that she struggled with her eating, I started to think that we should be focusing on that and began to lose the thread of what we were discussing. I started to think about how to encourage the client to come back so we could deal with her eating issue.

SST supervisor: What happened?

Therapist: We got to the end of the session and the client thanked me for seeing her.

SST supervisor: What did the client say she was going to take away from the session?

Therapist: I forgot to ask. To be honest with you I was in a bit of turmoil by the end.

SST supervisor: What was the turmoil about?

Therapist: Well, I was torn between maintaining the SST mindset and focusing on the issue the client wanted to discuss and dealing with her eating issue because that seemed more damaging to her.

SST supervisor: How do you think you can resolve the conflict?

Therapist: I have been thinking about that. I think I need to place more emphasis in my mind on the SST principle of the client leading the session. She only mentioned her issues with eating in passing and although they did seem troubling to me, they did not seem troubling to her.

SST supervisor: Maybe you could remember that phrase, 'What seems troubling to me may not be troubling to the client'.

Therapist: That's a really good idea.

SST supervisor: Can you imagine reminding yourself of that before you go into an SST session?

Therapist: Yes, I can.

SST supervisor: What difference would that make to you?

Therapist: It would keep my focus on what the client finds troubling and wants help with.

Listening to Recordings

The advantage of the therapist playing a recording of an SST therapy session in supervision is that the supervisor gets to hear the actual work that the therapist has done with a client and not just a verbal account of that session. From the present perspective, the major task of the supervisor is to listen for instances that the therapist has moved away from doing SST and to explore the reasons for it. When this happens the supervisor engages the therapist in a similar dialogue to that presented above.

Developing Peer Support

One of the advantages of participating in a training course on SST with other trainees is that a person can be part of a peer-support community. The person can call upon this community in a number of ways. Thus, a therapist may team up with a trainee colleague to practice their skills in peer counselling.[1]

In the present context, therapists may call upon members of their community to discuss their difficulties with internalising the SST mindset and with their practice of SST.

---

1 In peer counselling one person serves as the therapist and the other as the client. The client brings up a genuine problem that they would like help with and the therapist works to help them with the issue. They then switch roles.

Being Mindful of the Difficulties One Has as an SST Therapist Before the Session

In my view it is important that therapists are honest with themselves about the difficulties they experience with SST and its implementation. Once discovering a difficulty, it is important that a therapist identifies a solution to this difficulty and has a way of implementing this solution while doing SST. An example of this process was presented in the exchange above between an SST therapist and their supervisor. Here the therapist admitted having difficulty focusing on the client's agenda because of their concern about an area of the client's life that the latter mentioned, but not as a matter of their own concern. The supervisor suggested to the therapist a pithy phrase[2] for the therapist to review before SST sessions so that they can be guided by it during sessions.

In my career as an SST therapist, I have experienced certain difficulties in doing SST and have developed a solution for each. The following are statements that I have used and the difficulties they were developed to address:

- 'Hit it and quit it'[3]

This means that once I have helped the client achieve their session goal (i.e., I have 'hit it') then it is time to bring the session to an end ('quit it'). I developed this phrase to alert me to my tendency of trying to help someone with a second problem once I had helped them with their first.

- 'Less is more'

'Less is more' is a feature of what I have referred to in this book as SST 'orientation' thinking (see Chapter 10). It runs counter to the belief in conventional therapy that the more you give a client, the better; what might be called 'more is more'. Many SST therapists find it hard to adjust to the idea that if you help a person take away from

---

2 'What seems troubling to me may not be troubling to the client'.
3 'Hit it and quit it' is a repeated lyric at the end of James Brown's 'Get up (I feel like being a) sex machine'.

the session one thing that may be meaningful that they implement in their life then this makes for a successful session (Keller & Papasan, 2012). I really struggled to do this at the beginning of my career as an SST therapist and still do, at times. So a gentle reminder that 'less is more' in single-session therapy helps me to orient myself to the session. Thus, I no longer cram too much into the session which I used to do when I first started to practise SST.

- 'Let the client's brain take the strain'

An old advert for British Rail[4] had the tag line, 'Let the train take the strain'. This was used to suggest to people that they could save themselves much strain by leaving their cars at home and use trains instead. Effective single-session therapy depends in part on the client thinking for themselves and being an active participant in the SST therapeutic relationship. Thus, SST therapists should ideally encourage their clients to use their brains as well as acting on what they have learned after the session. Hence, the phrase, 'Let the client's brain take the strain'.

However, given the possible length of SST, the therapist, as we have seen, is tempted to cover too much ground and thereby gives the client more than they can digest. When this happens, it is quite easy for the therapist to do a lot of the work for the client and thus, albeit unwittingly, encourage them to be mentally lazy, particularly when the therapist goes into didactic mode. Whenever possible, therefore, the therapist should work in a Socratic manner with the client. By doing so, they encourage the client to think through issues for themselves. This does not mean that at times the therapist should not make didactic explanations. However, when they do so, it is vital that they ask the client to put into their own words their understanding of what they, the therapist has been attempting to convey. Checking with the client in this way not only helps the client to be actively involved in the session, it also helps the therapist to get feedback on the clarity of their communications and then what the client thinks of the points being made.

Because my difficulties in practising SST were, and to some extent still are, in the realm of giving the client too much, I was (and am) also

---

4 British Rail, was a state-owned company that operated most of the overground rail transport in Great Britain from 1948 to 1997. It was privatised in 1997 and the rail network is now run by a number of companies and franchises.

prone to doing too much work for the client. So, a gentle reminder before I start the session to let my 'client's brain take the strain' does not go amiss.

To help novice SST therapists remember core principles of SST in a pithy form, I published *The SST Therapist's Pocket Companion* (Dryden, 2022c). I partly wrote the book to help therapists remind themselves of aspects of SST with which they have difficulty. I say this in the book's introduction: '... if you discover an area of SST where you struggle, my hope is that you may find something in this book that might help you deal productively with your struggle in an easily remembered form. As such, the book is designed to be kept in your pocket so that you can consult it when you need a timely reminder of a point of good SST practice' (Dryden, 2022c: v).

Using the Client's Pre-Session Form to Prepare for the Session

As discussed in Chapter 15, the main purpose of the client completing the pre-session questionnaire sent to them by the therapist in independent practice or the agency in which the therapist works is for the client to prepare for the session so that they can get the most from it. They are also invited to send a copy of the completed form back to the therapist so that the therapist can prepare for the session as well.

Not all SST therapists like to prepare for the session by reading what the client has written on their pre-session questionnaire. Such therapists prefer to do SST knowing nothing about the client because they want to be free of any preconceptions while working the client (see Chapter 3). However, many SST therapists do like to know what is in the client's mind before the session particularly with respect to what they want to achieve from the session. Their view is that some of the client's responses provide information that the therapist would have asked for in the session (e.g., strengths, external resources and previous attempts to solve the problem), thus saving both time that can be better spent in the session.

So, reviewing the client's responses on the pre-session questionnaire is another way that the therapist can prepare themself for the session. I would add one caveat here. It is important for the therapist to check that the client's responses have not changed when beginning the session. Sometimes, for example, the client changes their mind about how to use the session and the therapist should be aware of such a possibility (see Chapter 3 for an example of when the client does have such a change of mind).

Part III

SST 'In-Session' Thinking

In this final part of the book, I will focus on the third part of the SST mindset – SST 'in-session' thinking. Here, I will consider different elements of the SST process from the beginning of the session to the follow-up phase. In doing so, I will use constructed dialogue between the client and the SST therapist to highlight the latter's in-session and show how this influences their interventions in the session.

While different clients do require different helping stances from SST therapists (see Chapter 19), by far the most frequently requested form of help is for the therapist to assist the client in dealing with an emotional/behavioural problem with which the client is stuck. Given this, I will focus on this form of help in this part of the book.

DOI: 10.4324/9781032657752-20

Chapter 17

Beginning the Session

Beginning the session in SST depends on what has gone on before the therapist and client meet to have the session. Here are a number of considerations:

- Are the therapist and client having the session in the therapist's independent practice or in an agency in which the therapist works? If the therapist is practicing SST in an agency, that organisation may have procedures that they require the therapist to follow at the outset of therapy even in SST. This will affect how the therapist begins the SST session.
- What does the client know about SST? In agencies that offer SST, information about SST is made available on their websites and via online applications for help. However, this does not mean that a client has read this material and it may be the case they come to the session with unrealistic expectations.
- Have the client and therapist had any contact prior to the session? In agencies that offer SST, it may be that the first time that the therapist and client meet is at the beginning of the SST session. This has a decided bearing on how the therapist begins the session.
- Has the client completed any pre-session questionnaire? If so, have they returned it to the therapist before they meet? If the client has completed and returned the form, then this gives the therapist the opportunity to use some of the information contained therein to begin the session.

Table 17.1 lists common scenarios and how the SST therapist can begin the session in light of each scenario.

DOI: 10.4324/9781032657752-21

Table 17.1 Scenarios and Beginning Strategies in SST

Scenario	Beginning Strategy
• The therapist and client are meeting in the therapist's independent practice	• The therapist is free to begin the session in any way they choose
• The therapist and client are meeting in an agency	• The therapist needs to begin the session with procedures mandated by the agency
• The client has an accurate understanding of SST	• The therapist is free to begin the session in any way they choose
• The client does not have an accurate understanding of SST	• The therapist begins by explaining what SST is and what it is not
• The therapist and client have had prior contact	• The therapist uses their prior contact to begin the session
• The therapist and client have had no prior contact	• The therapist introduces themself and finds out what the client knows about SST and proceeds accordingly
• The client has completed and returned the pre-session questionnaire	• The therapist can begin by referring to the questionnaire
• The client has not completed or returned the pre-session questionnaire	• The therapist begins by finding out what the client knows about SST and proceeds accordingly

Eliciting Informed Consent

In Chapter 14, I discussed in general terms the issue of eliciting informed consent with clients in single-session therapy. In the example below I will show how a therapist elicited informed consent from a client who had faulty expectations of the work that the two of them were about to embark on together.

SST therapist: Before we begin, what is your understanding of what we are going to do today?

Client: Well, I was told that we would have a one-off therapy session.

[SST therapist's thinking: I need to find out what the client means by a 'one-off' therapy session. I suspect that they mean that no further help would be available to them which is incorrect. If so, I will have to correct this misconception.]

SST therapist: What do you mean by a one-off therapy session?

Client: That I will have one therapy session and that is that.

SST therapist: That is not the case. Many people think that the term single-session therapy means that, but it doesn't. It means that I will strive to help you today with whatever you wish to discuss with me, but that more help is available for you in the future if you think you need it.

Client: So, I'm not restricted to one session?

[SST therapist's thinking: I will have to have a word with the administrator of the agency where I work. It may be that clients are being given inaccurate information by agency personnel, although it is accurate on the website.]

SST therapist: Not at all. You may not need more than one session, but you are not restricted to one session.

Client: That sounds better.

SST therapist: So, would you like to proceed on that basis?

Client: Yes, I would.[1]

SST therapist: Can I check something with you before we start. Did you look at the 'Single-Session Therapy' page on our website?

Client: No, I don't use the internet much.

SST Therapist: So, who told you about single-session therapy.

---

1 Gaining a client's informed consent is one aspect of contracting. Other issues including agreeing confidentiality and other practical issues are done in SST. See Chapter 14.

Client: A nice young lady did when I telephoned the agency.

[SST therapist's thinking: I will definitely have to speak to the administrator about this issue. It may be that the staff who speak to prospective clients need retraining about SST and how to explain it to people when they call.]

Beginning the Session if the Client Has Completed and Returned the Pre-Session Preparation Form

In Chapter 15, I discussed that before they have the session, the client is often invited to prepare for the session by completing a pre-session questionnaire which they are asked to return to the therapist who can also prepare for the session. When the client has completed and returned such a form, at the very least the therapist needs to thank the client for doing so and asks them for permission to refer to the form if necessary during the session. However, the therapist could also use the form to begin the session.

SST therapist: Thank you for completing the pre-session questionnaire.

Client: You're welcome.

SST therapist: Would you mind if I refer to the questionnaire, if necessary, in the session?

Client: Not at all.

[SST therapist's thinking: It may be that filling in the form has prompted some kind of change in the person. I'll start by enquiring whether this is the case.]

SST therapist: Thanks. Now, what changes, if any, have you noticed between completing the questionnaire and the session today?

The therapist proceeds according to the client's response to this question. If the client has noticed any changes, then the therapist would begin with this and help them both understand what occasioned the change and how this could be capitalised upon. On the other hand, if the client has not noticed any changes, then the therapist would ask a question taken from one of the following sections. Here is an example of the latter.

> *SST therapist*: Thanks. Now, what changes, if any, have you noticed between completing the questionnaire and the session today?
>
> *Client*: I haven't noticed any changes.
>
> *[SST therapist's thinking: OK, so I think I will continue by refer-ring to what the client wrote in response to the question about what they want to achieve from the session.]*
>
> *SST therapist*: OK, now you say on the form that you want to get some tips and techniques about how to deal with your anxiety. Is that correct?
>
> *Client*: Yes.
>
> *[SST therapist's thinking: I just need to check that this is still current before proceeding.[2]]*
>
> *SST therapist*: Is that still the case?
>
> *Client*: Yes.
>
> *SST therapist*: OK, now do you think it is best for us to proceed on our quest for those tips and techniques based on a full under-standing of your anxiety or without such an understanding?
>
> *Client*: We need to understand my anxiety first, I would have thought.
>
> *SST therapist*: I agree. So, let's make a start with understanding your anxiety.[3]

2 As noted in Chapters 3 and 16, clients occasionally change their mind about how they want to use the session between them completing the pre-session questionnaire and the session itself.

3 A solution-focused, single-session therapist would probably not take this tack because it means focusing on the client's problem. My own approach to SST is problem-solution-goal focused (see Dryden, 2023a) and this is reflected in the present book.

Beginning the Session by Focusing on Its Purpose

As I have already mentioned, many therapy agencies are interested in introducing SST into their service provision in order to reduce waiting lists. However, while SST has this *effect,* its therapeutic *intent* is, as has already been discussed, to provide help at the point of need and to see if therapists can help clients achieve their therapeutic goals in a single session, knowing that more help can be accessed, if needed. Given that SST has a therapeutic purpose, this can form a good way of beginning the session. When the therapist asks the client about their understanding of the purpose of the session they discover quickly if the client has a realistic view of the purpose of SST or not. If not, the therapist can be clear about they can do and what they can't do, helping the orient the client to the therapeutic potency of SST. Here are two examples where the focus on the purpose of SST yields a realistic response (Example 1) and an unrealistic response (Example 2) and how the SST therapist responds in each case.

Example 1

SST therapist: From your perspective, what is the purpose of our conversation today?

Client: The purpose is that we are going to have a session and you are going to try to help me deal with my problem and if I need more help, I can have it.

SST therapist: That is exactly right. So, let's get down to work.

Example 2

SST therapist: From your perspective, what is the purpose of our conversation today?

Client: You are going to assess me and see if I need ongoing counselling.

[SST therapist's thinking: I obviously need to find out if that is what the client is looking for. I also need to find out where the client got this impression from, but first things first.]

SST therapist: Is that the service you are looking for?

Client: To be honest, I'm not sure.

[SST therapist's thinking: That's encouraging. At least, I am not going to have to tell the person that I don't offer the help that they want.]

SST therapist: Well, the service that I offer to which you have been referred is called single-session therapy. This means that you and I would work together to help you to take away something from the session that will make a difference to your life. This session may be all you need at this time, or you may need more help which we can provide. We find that about half the people who use this service are helped in this one session and half request more help. We don't know in advance though who will fit into which group. We only find out that at the end. What do you think?

Client: So, you will be helping me today rather than assessing me, is that right?

SST therapist: That is right.

Client: And I can have more help if I need it after today?

SST therapist: Yes, you can.

Client: Then I'm happy with that.

[SST therapist's thinking: Before I take that as the client's informed consent, I want to give them an opportunity to ask any questions about what I have said.]

SST therapist: Do you have any other questions about the service that I provide?

Client: No.

> *SST therapist*: So, are you happy to go forward on the understanding that we will work together to help you today and you can have more help later if you need it?
>
> *Client*: Yes, I'm happy to do that.

Beginning the Session by Asking about the Client's Problem/Issue/Concern

As most clients seek SST for help with a problem, issue or concern,[4] another common way of beginning SST is for the therapist to be problem focused.[5] For example:

> *Therapist*: What problem, concern or issue would you like to discuss with me?

or

> *Therapist*: What problem, concern or issue would you like me to help you with?

Sometimes, the client wants help with more than one problem for SST. In the two examples below, note the different ways in which the SST therapist responds to this scenario.

Example 1

SST therapist: What problem would like me to help you with?

Client: I have been thinking about that. I'm anxious about three things. I'm anxious about giving presentations at work, eating

---

4 Different therapists, and clients, have their own preferences about what to call the difficulty for which the client seeking help. From a working alliance perspective it is productive for the therapist and client to use agreed terminology here.

5 Again, a therapist who practises SST from a solution-focused perspective would probably decide *not* to ask a problem-focused question at the outset as they would want to be solution-focused in their questioning.

out in front of my girlfriend's parents and my hands shaking when drinking from a cup and saucer.

[SST therapist's thinking: I won't have time to help the person with all three of their problems, so let me ask them to prioritise.]

SST therapist: We probably won't have time to deal with all of these, which one of these problems would you like to focus on today?

Client: Giving presentations at work.

Example 2

SST therapist: What problem would like me to help you with?

Client: I have been thinking about that. I'm anxious about three things. I'm anxious about giving presentations at work, eating out in front of my girlfriend's parents and my hands shaking when drinking from a cup and saucer.

[SST therapist's thinking: I won't have time to help the person with all three of their problems, but let me see if there is a common theme that might help me to deal with one and help the person generalise their learning to the other two.]

SST therapist: We probably won't have time to deal with all of these. However, do you see any connection between them?

Client: Well, they all seem connected to me and reveal something negative about myself in a public setting.

SST therapist: I was thinking the same thing. One way of proceeding today is for you to select one of these three problems that we can discuss in greater detail. However, as we do so we keep the theme in mind so that if I can help you with the problem you choose, you may be able to generalise what you learn to the other two problems. Is that a good way forward?

Client: Yes, it is.

SST therapist: So, which of the three problems you mentioned would it be best for us to focus on today?

Client: Giving presentations at work.

Let me say that in the above two examples, I would suggest that the less experienced SST therapist adopts the 'let's focus on one problem' approach and the second 'let's focus on the theme' approach is taken only by the more experienced SST therapist.

There are two other ways in which the SST therapist could begin the session: i) by asking the client what goal they want to achieve and ii) by asking the client what helping stance they want the therapist to take in the session. However, my own view is that these two issues are dealt with after the therapist has initiated the session by taking one of the approaches previously discussed. Consequently, I will deal with helping the client to nominate a goal in Chapter 18 and helping them to nominate what helping stance they think will be most helpful to them in Chapter 19.

Helping the Client to Nominate a Goal

Therapy is a goal-directed activity and in SST we are clear that the client sets their own goal. In my experience there are two goals that are relevant to SST. These can be referred to as the session goal and the problem-related goal. As I discussed in Chapter 7, a session goal is what the client wants to achieve by the end of the session and a problem-related goal is what the person wants to achieve with respect to their nominated problem. The relationship between the two is shown in the following diagram which also appears in Chapter 7.

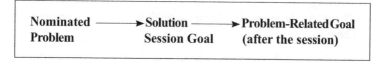

This diagram shows that what the client wants to achieve by the end of the session often serves as the solution to their nominated problem. It also shows that the client needs to implement the solution after the session in order to achieve their problem-related goal.

Given that the emphasis in SST is on helping the client to achieve their stated wants from the session, the therapist needs to help them to state these wants. These will serve as their session goals. However, if the client expresses a problem-related goal, the therapist needs to be clear about what they can do (help the client to take a few steps towards achieving their problem-related goal) and what they can't do (help them achieve their problem-related goal by the end of the session).

DOI: 10.4324/9781032657752-22

Helping the Client to Nominate a Session Goal

It can be difficult to help a client to set a session goal, as will be demonstrated in the following example.

SST therapist: What would you like to achieve by talking with me today?[1]

Client: I would like to deal with my anxiety.

[SST therapist's thinking: The client's answer is a bit vague, so I am going to see if I can help them to be more specific.]

SST therapist: Your anxiety about what?

Client: Mainly about my health.

[SST therapist's thinking: I think I need to ask for a specific example so I can help the client find a specific session goal.]

SST therapist: Can you perhaps give me a specific example?

Client: At the moment I have a cough and am very anxious about it.

SST therapist: If you were dealing with the cough in a healthy way, what would you be feeling and doing that would be different?

Client: Good question. I have always thought that my goal would be not to be anxious about my health, but your question has made me think… (pause)… I think I would like to be healthily anxious about my health and not unhealthily about it, if that makes sense.

SST therapist: Yes, it does. If you were healthily anxious about your health, what would you be doing that is different than you are doing now?

Client: I would be more patient and wait to see what happens with my cough. At the moment I have consulted two doctors and

---

1 An alternative goal-related question here would be: 'What would you like to take away from our conversation that would make it worthwhile that you came today?'.

rang the NHS helpline. I have also been 'googling' coughs. If I was healthily anxious, I wouldn't be doing any of these things.

[SST therapist's thinking: I have now got the client's problem-related goal. I now have to explain that I won't be able to help the client to achieve all this by the end of the session, but I can offer them the means to do this after the session has finished.]

SST therapist: Would it be helpful if I make clear what I think I can do in the session today and what I can't do so that we are both on the same page about where we are going in the session?

Client: That would be useful.

SST therapist: You have stipulated what you want to achieve in relation to your problem. You want to feel healthily anxious about your health rather than unhealthily anxious. I can't help you to achieve this by the end of the session. What I can do today is work with you to discover a way of achieving your problem-related goal which you can implement after the session in your own life. Would that be of interest to you?

Client: Definitely.

In the above example, the SST therapist did the following. They helped the client be specific about their nominated problem (health anxiety). They helped the client specify a problem-related goal (be healthily anxious and not unhealthily anxious about health and act accordingly) and a session goal (find the means to achieve their problem-related goal). Put diagrammatically, we have:

Health →	**Discover Means** →	**Healthily Anxious**
Anxiety	**to be Healthily**	**About Health**
Nominated	**Anxious About**	Problem-Related
Problem	**Health**	Goal
	Solution/Session Goal	(after the session)

Chapter 19

Discovering What Help the Client Is Seeking from the Therapist

While most clients seem to want help to solve an emotional or behavioural problem in SST,[1] other forms of help are available, and soon after the therapist has begun the session, it is useful to ask the client about the type of help they are seeking from the therapist. Questions that the therapist can ask on this point include:

- 'How can I be most helpful to you today?'
- 'What help would you like from me today?'

If the client struggles to answer the question initially, then the therapist should give them alternatives, as shown below.

SST therapist: What help would you like from me today?

Client: I'm not sure.

[SST therapist's thinking: I will list all the ways of helping that I can provide and see if this helps the client to get some clarity about what help they are looking for.]

SST therapist: Well, there are several ways in which I could be helpful. Would you like me to summarise them, and you can tell me which one resonates most with what you think would be most helpful?

Client: That would be useful.

---

1 In the introduction to this part of the book, I explained that given this fact, I will be focusing on this form of help in SST in outlining how SST therapists think and intervene.

DOI: 10.4324/9781032657752-23

SST therapist: Well, I could help you to develop a greater understanding of an issue; I could just listen while you talk about an issue; I could help you to express your feelings about an issue; I could help you to solve an emotional or behavioural problem with which you feel stuck; I could help you to make a decision if that were relevant, I could help you resolve a dilemma; I could offer my professional opinion about something or I can help signpost you to get more extensive help. Do any of these describe the kind of help you are looking for?

It may be that by the time the therapist comes to ask about the client's preferred therapist 'helping stance', the therapist is clearer about what the client is looking for, and therefore the list they offer the client will be truncated.

Sometimes a client may ask for a form of help that the therapist may be reluctant to give. In this case, it is important that the therapist is transparent about what they are prepared to do and what they are not prepared to do as in the following.

SST therapist: How can I be most helpful to you today?

Client: I would like you to give me some advice about which job offer to take.

[SST therapist's thinking: It is not my job to give the client advice, so I need to be clear about that. However, I also need to be clear about what I can offer the client.]

SST therapist: Well, therapy is very different from advice-giving. So, I won't do that. However, I would be more than happy to look with you at the job options you have and help you to figure out which course of action to take based on what's important to you rather than on what I think you should do. How does that sound?

Client: That sounds OK.

When a client nominates a helping stance like 'understanding an issue' or 'expressing my feelings about an issue', they may just want that particular form of help and no other, or they may implicitly hope that being helped in this way will lead them to solve a problem. I will provide an example of both.

Example 1

SST therapist: How can I be most helpful to you today with respect to your health anxiety?

Client: I want to understand why I have this problem of health anxiety.

[SST therapist's thinking: I am not clear whether the client means they are looking for a historical reason or what factors in the present account for their problem. I need clarity on this point.]

SST therapist: Do you mean you are looking for historical reasons why you have this problem or that you would like to understand what factors in the present account for the problem?

Client: I want to understand what factors in the present account for this problem.

[SST therapist's thinking: Now I need to find out whether understanding is all they are looking for or are they hoping that such understanding will lead to something else.]

SST therapist: And if you understand the factors that account for your problem, what, if anything, do you hope that this understanding will do for you?

Client: I am hoping that it will help me find a solution to my health anxiety problem.

[SST therapist's thinking: I am wondering if the client sees that they will need my help with finding a solution or whether they think that they can find it on their own. I will ask them now.]

SST therapist: Once you understand the factors do you think that you will be able to find the solution, or do you think you will need my help for that?

Client: I will need your help with that.

Example 2

SST therapist: How can I be most helpful to you today?

Client: I feel all pent up with emotion, and I would like you to help me to express my feelings.

[SST therapist's thinking: I need to discover if the client wants just to express their feelings or whether they hope that this will lead to some other kind of help. So, I will now ask them this.]

SST therapist: And if you are able to express your feelings, what do you hope this will do for you?

Client: Well, I know from past experience that when I express my feelings, I can look at whatever it is with greater clarity, and that helps me to put things into perspective.

[SST therapist's thinking: The client is quite clear that emotional expression helps them to gain clarity, and this, in turn, helps them to put things into perspective. What I am not clear about is whether they see that I can be helpful in the 'gaining clarity, putting things into perspective process or if they can do that for themself without my help. I will check this now.]

SST therapist: So, once I have helped you to express your feelings, do you see a role for me in helping you to gain clarity and to put things into perspective or will you be able to do that on your own?

Client: I can do that by myself. The help I need from you is to help me express my feelings about what is going on in my life.

SST therapist: OK, that's fine. Tell me what's going on in your life and I'll help you express your feelings.

Helping Stances in SST Reviewed

As mentioned in one of the therapist's responses to a client above, there are several ways in which a therapist can help their client is SST. Thus, a therapist can help the client:

- to express their feelings about an issue;
- by listening while the client talks about an issue;
- to gain greater understanding of an issue;
- to solve an emotional/behavioural problem with which they feel stuck;
- to make a decision;
- to resolve a dilemma;
- to offer a professional opinion about an issue; and
- to provide signposting assistance to other services.

The most important point here is that the therapist offers the type of help that the client wants (Norcross & Cooper, 2021). This serves to strengthen the working alliance between therapist and client.

When a Client's Nominated Helping Stance Will Not Help, in All Probability

As I have mentioned on several occasions, SST is client-led. In the present context this means that the therapist helps the client to specify their preferred helping stance and, unless there is a good reason not to do so, the therapist will provide that stance. However, in my experience, sometimes there is a reason for the therapist to question the client's preferred helping stance because in the therapist's professional view, such a stance won't yield the results the client hopes it will. This is particularly the case when the client thinks that simply gaining insight into a problem or expressing their feelings about a problem will help change a habit-based specific problem, when they probably won't.

In my view, being client-led does not mean that the therapist stays silent in such situations. The therapist has a voice and needs to use it to provide a contrary view. Now, the client has every right to reject this view and I am not advocating that the therapist should impose their expertise on the client. What I am saying is that the therapist has expertise and needs to share it especially when the client harbours a misconception such as 'expressing my feelings on its own will change a habit-based specific issue'.

Let me provide an example of this where the client wants to deal with their nominated jealousy problem and wants the therapist to help them to understand the roots of this problem, believing that doing so will solve the issue for them.

SST therapist: So, in this session you want to deal with your jealousy issue. What way of helping you with this do you think will be most productive for you?

Client: I want you to help me to understand where this jealousy problem comes from.

[SST therapist's thinking: I need to clarify whether the client means the origins of this problem or the present factors that account for it.]

SST therapist: By 'understanding where your jealousy problem comes from', do you mean the origins of it or what factors drive it in the present?

Client: I mean the origins of it, where it comes from originally.

[SST therapist's thinking: That is what I feared the client meant. I hope the client thinks that getting this understanding of the origins of their problem will be useful if it helps them understand and deal with the present factors and is not sufficient. I need to check first.]

SST therapist: And if I helped you understand the origins your jealousy problem, what difference do you think that will make to you?

Client: If I understand it then I won't be jealous anymore.

[SST therapist's thinking: That is not the case, and I am going to have to be clear with the client about this. I am going to take a leaf out of Jeff Young's (2024) work on 'No Bullshit Therapy' and marry honesty and directness with warmth and care.]

SST therapist: I really want you to help you address your jealousy problem today. I can see how miserable you are, but can I level with you about something?

Client: OK.

SST therapist: While considering the past origins of your jealousy may have merit, in my therapeutic experience, on its own it is not going to solve your jealousy problem.

Client: OK, that's interesting. What is?

SST therapist: In my view, looking at your currently held attitudes towards such issues as the threats you perceive to your relationship, uncertainty, your partner and yourself and the behaviours that flow from these attitudes is really important. Unless we address these, I fear your jealousy problem will continue.

Client: OK, I see what you mean, I'm happy to go along with doing that.

Chapter 20

Creating a Focus and Maintaining It

Apart from the situation where a client wants to use the session to talk and for the therapist to listen while they talk, the work of the single-session therapist is to co-create a focus with the client. This focus may be problem-oriented, solution-oriented, goal-oriented or a combination of the three.

Helping the Client to Create a Focus

In Chapters 17 and 18, I covered the process of problem nomination and goal elicitation, the outcome of which yields naturally to the focus for the session. However, rather than make this assumption, it is useful for the therapist to check this with the client.

For completeness, let me give an example of how the therapist can help the client select a solution-oriented focus for the session.

SST therapist: You said on your pre-session form that you were hoping to learn some tips and techniques to help with anxiety. Is that still current for you?

Client: Yes, can you help me to do that?

[SST therapist's thinking: I need to see if the client can accept my proposal to base this search for 'tips and techniques' on a full understanding of their anxiety.]

SST therapist: I think I can best do that if I first help both of us get a full understanding of the factors that account for your anxiety. Does that make sense?

Client: Yes, as long we get round to the tips and techniques.

DOI: 10.4324/9781032657752-24

> *SST therapist*: We will. So, can we agree that the focus of the session will be on us looking for ways of helping you to deal with your anxiety based on a full understanding of it?
>
> *Client*: Agreed.

Helping the Client to Maintain the Agreed Focus

Once the therapist and client have agreed on a focus, it is vital for both to maintain this focus if the client is to get the most from the session. Having said that, in my view, it is the therapist's primary task to make sure that they both maintain the agreed focus is maintained. The therapist does this in several ways.

Seeking and Gaining Permission to Interrupt the Client

In my initial training course (in 1974–5). I was taught that it was bad practice to interrupt the client. The therapist's primary task was to facilitate the client's exploration of their concerns and to follow them in this exploration rather than provide any direction. Consequently, we as trained therapists had no reason to interrupt the client, since there was no agreed focus to maintain in the session. Aside from this, interrupting the client was seen as being rude.

In single-session therapy, interrupting is regarded very differently. Once the therapist and client have agreed a focus for the session, the therapist needs to take the lead in making sure that this focus is maintained during the session. As the client *may* view the therapist interrupting them as being rude, the therapist first provides a rationale for interrupting the client and then asks for their permission to do so. Here is an example:

> *SST therapist*: So now we have agreed on a focus for the session, we both need to maintain this focus. OK?
>
> *Client*: OK.

[SST therapist's thinking: Now I need to give a clear rationale for interrupting the client and get their permission to interrupt them.]

SST therapist: In any social conversation between two people, it is natural for one or both of them to range from topic to topic, and that is quite OK because there is no reason for them to stay with one topic. However, in a therapeutic conversation, when you and I agree have agreed on a focus, ranging from topic to topic is problematic. So, if that happens with us today, I would like to interrupt you to bring us back to the focus. My hope is to do so as sensitively as I can, but I will need to do this. Do I have your permission to do so?

Client: Yes, that is fine. I do find it difficult to keep to the point.

SST therapist: Thank you. Please feel free to interrupt me if I go off topic too.

Client: [laughing] I will.

Checking that Both Are Maintaining the Focus

Sometimes it is difficult for the therapist to be certain about whether or not a client has wandered away from an agreed focus. Thus, what may seem initially to be a departure from the focus, may be an important elaboration on a topic that clarifies the focus. As mutual dialogue is a key feature in SST, when this occurs, the therapist needs to check with the client that the focus is being maintained. Here is an example:

Client: That reminds me of something else. My wife agreed to stay at home tonight, but she tells me this morning that, once again, she is going out with her sister.

[SST therapist's thinking. Our agreed focus is on the client's anxiety about his son's schooling and now he is talking about their wife spending time with her sister. I need to see if these are connected or whether the client has departed arbitrarily from the focus and needs to be brought back to it.]

> *SST therapist*: Can I just check something with you?
>
> *Client*: OK.
>
> *SST therapist*: We agreed to focus on your anxiety about your son's schooling, and I am aware that we are now discussing your wife spending time with her sister. Is this connected to your anxiety about your son's schooling?
>
> *Client*: No, I'm sorry. I was going off track.
>
> *SST therapist*: No problem. Shall we get back to your feelings of anxiety about your son not getting into his preferred school?
>
> *Client*: Yes.

In the above dialogue, the client acknowledges that they had gone off track. The following is an example where what seems to be a departure from the focus, in fact, clarifies the focus.

> *Client*: And another thing. My daughter just does not seem to be getting on very well at the ballet school she is attending.
>
> *[SST therapist's thinking. Our agreed focus is on the client's anxiety about his son's schooling and now he is talking about his daughter's problems at her ballet school. I need to see if these are connected or whether the client has departed arbitrarily from the focus and needs to be brought back to it.]*
>
> *SST therapist*: Can I just check something with you?
>
> *Client*: Sure.
>
> *SST therapist*: We agreed to focus on your anxiety about your son's schooling, and I am aware that we are now discussing your daughter's problems at ballet school. I am not sure how that fits with your anxiety about your son's schooling.
>
> *Client*: The way I see it, they are both instances of my anxiety that my children may be blocked in getting what they really want in life.

> *SST therapist*: OK, I get that. They are linked. Would it make sense for us to maintain the focus on your son and then see if I can help you to generalise whatever you learn to the situation with your daughter?
>
> *Client*: If we could do both today, that would be great.
>
> *SST therapist*: OK, let's do that.

In this latter exchange, the client's apparent departure from the agreed focus (anxiety about the client's son schooling) turned out to be a clarification of the focus (anxiety about the client's children not getting what they really want in life). The former is a specific example of the latter, and the client's introduction of his daughter was another specific example of the broader focus. Note how the therapist acknowledged the connection and made the suggestion that they remain with the specific instance of the now broadened focus (anxiety about the client's son's schooling). The therapist then indicated that the client could generalise any learning to the other particular instance of the broadened focus (anxiety about the client's daughter's difficulties at ballet school).

This latter example shows how the single-session therapist works with both the specific and the general in SST. When there is a connection between the two, the SST therapist ensures that both can be discussed in the session. Having said that, the emphasis is usually on the specific and then the client can be helped to generalise any learning derived from that specific focus to other relevant situations.

Checking in with the Client Even When the Focus Is Being Maintained

Even when both therapist and client are maintaining the agreed therapeutic focus, it is important for the therapist to check periodically with the client that they are still talking about what they want to talk about. If not, and there is time to do so, then they can begin to discuss what is more important to the client and work towards a newly set session goal.

Chapter 21

Understanding the Problem

Once the therapist and client have agreed on which of the latter's problems they are going to focus on in the session,[1] it is important for them both to understand the problem.[2] There are a number of important issues that come to the fore when understanding the client's problem in SST, which I will discuss in this session. These are:

- Eliciting the client's view of the problem and what accounts for it.
- Offering a therapy-informed view of the problem and what accounts for it.
- Understanding the problem in context.
- Working with a specific example of the problem (past or future?).
- Understanding how the client unwittingly maintains the problem.

Eliciting the Client's View of the Problem and What Accounts for It

One of the key tenets of single-session therapy is for the therapist to utilise client factors while helping them to achieve their stated wants from SST. In understanding the client's nominated problem, therefore, it is important for the therapist to elicit the client's view of the problem and what accounts for it. In this respect, it is important to note that clients vary quite considerably with respect to their understanding of their nominated problem. Some have a very vague notion of what their problem is while others have quite a detailed understanding of it.

---

1 I refer to this problem as the client's 'nominated' problem.
2 SST therapists with a solution-focused orientation would probably not do this.

DOI: 10.4324/9781032657752-25

In the following example, the client knows very little about their problem.

SST therapist: So, we have agreed to focus on your public-speaking anxiety. Agreed?

Client: That's right.

SST therapist: What is your view of the factors that explain why you are anxious about speaking in public?

Client: I'm not sure. It stems back to when I was at school, and I saw a friend of mine give a talk in class. He wasn't very good at it and I felt sorry for him and ever since then I became anxious about speaking in public and have avoided it whenever I can.

[SST therapist's thinking: So, the client learned something at the time arising from seeing his friend struggle while giving a talk. The client does not mention what he learned so let me see if I can help them to articulate this.]

SST therapist: What do you think you learned from watching your friend not being good at giving a talk in class that might help to explain your own anxiety about public speaking?

Client: I don't know. I try not to think about it.

[SST therapist's thinking: It seems that the client is really quite avoidant about their problem. Let me see if they have done any research on public-speaking. My guess is that the answer is 'no'.]

SST therapist: Some people 'google' their problem in order to find out more about it. Have you done anything similar?

Client: No, I haven't. As I say I try not to think about it.

[SST therapist's thinking: I think that the client may benefit from hearing my take on the subject. Let's see.]

> *SST therapist*: Would it be useful for you to hear my take on the factors that may account for anxiety?[3]
>
> *Client*: Very much so.

In the following example, the client has a partial understanding of their problem.

> *SST therapist*: So, we have agreed to focus on your public-speaking anxiety. Agreed?
>
> *Client*: That's right.
>
> *SST therapist*: What is your view of the factors that explain why you are anxious about speaking in public?
>
> *Client*: I have done quite a bit of research on this. What resonates with me is that I am anxious about others thinking that I am a fool if I say something foolish.
>
> *[SST therapist's thinking: That factor contributes to the client's public-speaking anxiety but doesn't fully account for it. Let me see what the client thinks about this.]*
>
> *SST therapist*: Do you think that this fully accounts for your anxiety?
>
> *Client*: Yes, I do.
>
> *[SST therapist's thinking: I am going to see if the client is interested in my take on the issue.]*
>
> *SST therapist*: I think you are partially right, but there are few other factors that are important. Would you like to hear my take on the issue?
>
> *Client*: Yes, please.

---

3 I have found it important to ask the client's permission for me to give my therapy-informed 'take' on their problem before I offer. They are unlikely to say 'no', but them saying 'yes' leads them, in my experience, to be more attentive than they otherwise might be.

Offering a Therapy-Informed View of the Problem and What Accounts for It

In my view, single-session therapy is a blend of what the client brings to the session and what the therapist brings to the session. One of things that the therapist brings to the session is what I call their therapy-informed view of the client's nominated problem and what accounts for it. As the two examples above show, it is important in SST for the therapist to enquire if the client is interested in this therapy-informed view of their problem before offering.it.

Here is how the therapist proceeded in the above example:

SST therapist: I think you are partially right, but there are few other factors that are important. Would you like to hear my take on the issue?

Client: Yes, please.

SST therapist: OK. So, let's go back to your prediction that others will think you are a fool if you say something foolish and let's suppose for the moment that you're correct. OK?

Client: Yes.

SST therapist: Now, it is clear that it is important to you that others don't think you are a fool if you say something foolish. Right?

Client: Right.

SST therapist: Now, which of the following two attitudes leads to your anxiety?

- Attitude 1: 'I don't want others to think that I am a fool if I say something foolish and if they do, they are right. I am a fool' or
- Attitude 2: 'I don't want others to think that I am a fool if I say something foolish and if they do, they are wrong. I am not a fool. I am an ordinary human being which can say foolish and non-foolish things'

Client: The first one leads to my anxiety.

SST therapist: And if you really believed the second attitude, how would you feel about talking in public?

Client: I would feel concerned about them thinking that I would be a fool if I said something foolish, but I wouldn't be anxious about it.

[SST therapist's thinking: I will now ask the client if they want to set concern as a goal with respect to speaking in public and if they do, I can offer Attitude 2 as the solution.]

SST therapist: What do you think of feeling concerned and not anxious with respect to speaking in public as a goal?

Client: I think that's a great idea.

SST therapist: And what do you think of developing Attitude 2 as a way of achieving this goal?

Client: That makes sense.

Understanding the Problem in Context

In preparing for the search for a solution to the client's nominated problem, it is useful for the therapist to help themselves and the client to understand the client's problem in context. In doing so, often important information is disclosed by the client that helps them develop a level of understanding, acceptance and self-compassion that may not be forthcoming without an understanding of this context. Here is an example:

SST therapist: So, let's see if we can both understand your problem with regret.[4] What regret do you want to focus on today?

Client: Choosing to study law rather than medicine.

---

4 The therapist had previously established that the client's regret was unhealthy in the sense that it was ruminative, self-blaming where the client thought that their life would be much better if they took the path that they now wished that had taken then.

SST therapist: When was this?

Client: Fifteen years ago.

[SST therapist's thinking: I am going to get as much information as I can so that I can help the client can see what they were thinking at the time.]

SST therapist: Tell me about that decision.

Client: Well, my father and uncle are lawyers and they suggested that I look into it as a career option.

SST therapist: And did you?

Client: Yes.

SST therapist: What did you decide?

Client: I thought that I would enjoy being a lawyer.

SST therapist: What led you to think that?

Client: I was interested in the concept of justice, and I liked the attention to detail. I also likes the salary I could achieve.

SST therapist: Did you have any doubts at that time about choosing the lawyer path?

Client: Not then, no.

[SST therapist's thinking: I am now going to ask the client about the thoughts that they had at the time concerning studying medicine rather than law, although I am pretty sure that this pathway had not occurred to them then. If I am right, I want the client to tell me this. It will have greater impact later if they do so.]

SST therapist: At the same time as you were thinking about becoming a lawyer, what were your thoughts about medicine as a career?

Client: I didn't have any.

[SST therapist: I am going to feign deafness and ask the client to repeat that. I want them to hear themself say that important point.]

SST therapist: I'm sorry I missed that. What did you say?

Client: I said I didn't have any.

SST therapist: Have any what?

Client: I didn't have any thoughts about becoming a doctor at that time.

SST therapist: So, let me get this clear. Fifteen years ago, You were seriously contemplating becoming a lawyer and at that time you had no doubts about making that decision. Also, at that time you had no thoughts at all about becoming a doctor. Is that right?

Client: Yes, and I get the point you are making.

[SST therapist's thinking: I am not making any point explicitly, but I am, of course, implicitly. I want the client to make this point rather than make it myself.]

SST therapist: Point?

Client: You are saying how could I regret my decision not to become a doctor fifteen years ago when I had no thoughts of doing so at that time.

[SST therapist's thinking: the client is partially right and partially wrong so I will need to make my point explicitly with respect to the difference between healthy and unhealthy envy.]

SST therapist: Yes and no. May I explain?

Client: Yes, please.

SST therapist: In my mind, there are two different types of regret: healthy regret and unhealthy regret.[5] In healthy regret, you look back and acknowledge that from the perspective of the present, you would have preferred to have become a doctor fifteen years ago rather than a lawyer, but you keep this preference flexible. This means that you also acknowledge that you did not have to decide to become a doctor at that time. It would have been desirable but not absolutely necessary. When you are in this

---

5 See Dryden (2023b).

flexible mindset, you are able to take advantage of the fact which was that there was no way you could have decided to become a doctor at that time because such a thought was not in your mind, and you are not demanding that it should have been in your mind at that time. Also, you acknowledge that there is no way of knowing how your life would have panned out if you had decided to become a doctor. It may have been better; it may have been worse, and it may have made no difference. You also acknowledge that you don't know how you would have taken to being a doctor: you may have liked it, you may have disliked it, or it may have been a mixture of the two. Basically, you accept yourself as an ordinary person who can only make decisions about things based on what is in your mind at the time. That's healthy regret.

Now, let me see if I have been clear. Can you put into your own words what I mean by healthy regret?[6]

Client: OK. You mean that it's OK to look back and regret a decision as long as you do so from a flexible mindset. This allows you to see the reality and not keep dwelling on what you did not do because you can see that you could not have done what you wished you had done. Also, you don't assume that your life would be better if you made a different decision. You are an ordinary person making decisions on what you know at the time.

SST therapist: That is a great summary. Now let me cover unhealthy regret. In unhealthy regret, you also look back and acknowledge that from the perspective of the present, you would have preferred to have become a doctor fifteen years ago rather than a lawyer. However, the difference is that you make this preference rigid. This means that you demand that you absolutely should have decided to become a doctor at that time. It was not just desirable but absolutely necessary. When you are in this rigid mindset, you can't see the fact which was that there was no way you could have decided to become a doctor at that time because such a thought was not in your mind.

---

6 Sometimes, in SST, the therapist does need to adopt an educational stance when explaining a complex point. Since the emphasis on SST is on client learning, it is important for the therapist to check that the client has understood the point that the therapist has made.

You are demanding that such a thought should have been in your mind at that time. You keep revisiting this point in your life and ruminating on why you did not do what you absolutely should have done. Also, you are convinced that your life would have turned out much better if you had decided to become a doctor. You think that you would have loved being a doctor. Basically, you blame yourself for not doing what you think you absolutely should have done. That's unhealthy regret.

Now, let me once again see if I have been clear. Can you put into your own words what I mean by unhealthy regret?

Client: OK. In unhealthy regret, when you look back and regret a decision, you do so from a rigid mindset. This does not allow you to see reality and leads you to keep dwelling on what you did not do and blame yourself for not doing it. You assume that your life would have better if you made a different decision.

SST therapist: Again, an excellent summary. Now which type of regret do you have about not becoming a doctor?

Client: Definitely unhealthy.

SST therapist: Would you like me to help you to have healthy rather than unhealthy regret?

Client: Definitely. Before speaking to you, I assumed that all regret is unhealthy, but you have helped me to see that there is a type of regret that is healthy.

[SST therapist's thinking: I want to see if the client has any reservations about healthy regret as a goal.]

SST therapist: Do you have any doubts, reservations or objections concerning working to make your regret healthy?

Client: Only if I can do it.

SST therapist: Well, are you willing to join me in finding out? What I can do is equip you with the solution to your unhealthy regret problem and help you to plan to implement it after we have finished today. Would that be of interest to you?

Client: Definitely.

By helping the client see their problem in context, the therapist was able to distinguish between healthy and unhealthy regret and show how elements of that contextual understanding can be incorporated into the solution to the client's problem. It is also important to note that the therapist helps the client to see what they can do in the session (i.e., equipping the client with a solution) and what they can't do (i.e., implementing that solution in the client's life).

Working with a Specific Example of the Problem

When a client nominates a problem for which they are seeking help, they usually express that problem in general terms. If the SST therapist works with the client's problem at a general level then two things are likely to happen. First, the therapist will get general rather than specific information from the client which will be less helpful to both of them as they strive to understand the specific factors involved in the client's problem. Second, the client will be less emotionally engaged emotionally in the conversation than they would be if they were both discussing a salient specific example. For these reasons, it is best if the therapist works with a specific example of the client's problem.

When inviting a client to discuss a specific example of their nominated problem, the therapist can ask the client to choose a past example of this problem or an anticipated example. The advantage of working with a past example of the client's problem is that as the episode has already occurred, the person can access i) the feelings they experienced in the situation and what these feelings were about, ii) the problem-related thoughts they had in the episode and iii) how they acted in the situation. The disadvantage of working with a past example is that whatever solution the client selects has to be implemented in an anticipated example of the client's problem. Contrast this with what happens when the therapist works with an anticipated example of the client's problem. Here, any solution can be implemented in the same situation as was selected by the client while discussing the episode with the therapist. The drawback in working with an anticipated example of the client's problem is that as the situation has not occurred, the client may not have clear information about how they may feel, think and act. The selection of a past or future specific example of the client's problem is largely in the hands of the client in SST.

Here is an example of an SST therapist working with a specific anticipated example of the client's problem:

SST therapist: So, the problem you want to focus on with me is your fear of criticism. Is that right?

Client: Yes.

[SST therapist's thinking: Let's see if I can encourage the client to come up with an anticipated example of their problem. First, I will need to give a rationale for this.]

SST therapist: Can you think of a situation that you want to face but avoid doing so because you fear criticism?

Client: I really need to get feedback from my tutor on my master's thesis. But I've been putting off doing so because I am afraid of her criticism.

SST therapist: The reason I suggested working with an anticipated example of your problem is that it is easier to implement a solution in the same situation as we have been discussing. However, if you wish we can discuss a past example of your fear of criticism.

Client: No, as I said I really need to get feedback from my tutor so let's deal with the future example.

SST therapist: OK so imagine that you have decided to get feedback from your tutor on your master's thesis. What are you most anxious about?

Client: Her saying that it is not master's level work, and it needs to be improved.

SST therapist: Would this feedback be given face-to-face, by Zoom or in an email?

Client: Face-to face.

SST therapist: If that happens, would your tutor give you feedback about how to improve your work or would she criticise it without giving you feedback?

Client: Oh no, she is very good at giving constructive feedback.

SST therapist: So, if you have to work on improving your thesis, what anxious meaning are you giving this situation?

Client: It means I am stupid.

[SST therapist's thinking: Let's see how the client would react if she had conviction in a healthier attitude towards herself in the face of this criticism from her tutor.]

SST therapist: Imagine for a moment, that your tutor criticised your work in this way, but that you really believed the following attitude: 'It's not pleasant having my thesis criticised, but it does not mean I'm stupid. It means that I am an ordinary person capable of doing good and not so good work. What difference would holding this attitude make to you?

Client: A great deal of difference. I would not be so afraid and I would be able to learn from the feedback.

SST therapist: Might this alternative attitude serve as a potential solution to your fear of criticism?

Client: For sure.

[SST therapist's thinking: I need to capitalise on the client's response by helping her to rehearse this attitude and trouble-shooting any blocks to her implementing it.]

Understanding How the Client Unwittingly Maintains the Problem

An important aspect of understanding a client's problem is for the therapist to help themselves and the client to discover how the client *unwittingly* maintains the problem. The goal is for the therapist to help them both identify the client's idiosyncratic maintenance factors so that the opposite of these factors can be used in the development of a workable solution to the client's nominated problem (see Chapter 22).

Table 21.1 How Clients Unwittingly Maintain Their Problems

- **Avoiding adversity**
- **Withdrawing from adversity**
- **Trying to eliminate the adversity or one's reaction to it**
- **Adopting a façade**
- **Seeking reassurance from others and from oneself**
- **Engaging in unhealthy behaviours (e.g., compulsions)**
- **Complying with others**
- **Being around others who have the same problem and legitimising it**
- **Not questioning unhealthy attitudes and thinking**
- **Distracting oneself from the problem**
- **Misusing substances (food, alcohol, drugs)**
- **Overcompensating for one's problem**
- **Disturbing oneself for the presence of the nominated problem (meta-problem)**
- **Knowing the solution but waiting for the presence of certain conditions to implement it**
- **Giving up once the problematic response has begun rather than productively responding to it**

There are numerous ways in which a client unwittingly maintains their nominated problem. I will briefly discuss the most common here and will show how an SST therapist works with a client to identify them. Table 21.1 outlines fifteen problem-maintenance factors. It is important for the SST therapist to have this framework in mind when working with the client to identify their idiosyncratic ways of unwittingly maintaining their nominated problem.

Avoiding Adversity

Perhaps the most common problem-maintaining factor is where the client avoids the adversity[7] that is at the heart of their problem. In doing that, they spare themself from experiencing their emotional problem, but do not get the experience that they need in facing the adversity and responding to it in a constructive way. SST can help the person discover that constructive way.

---

7 I think of an adversity as that aspect of a situation that the person finds most troubling. Thus, an adversity can be true or inferential. I have found that the best way to help a person to deal with an adversity in SST is to encourage them to think of it as true, at least temporarily.

Withdrawing from Adversity

The person may not avoid the adversity that is at the heart of their problem, but they may withdraw from it if they suspect that it may be occurring. Thus, a person who fears criticism may enter a situation where it may occur, but if it looks like it is going to occur, then they will leave the situation. Again, the SST therapist needs to help the person develop a constructive way of dealing with the adversity (in this case, criticism) and encourage them to stay in the situation to implement this solution.

Trying to Eliminate the Adversity or One's Reaction to It

A client may unwittingly maintain their nominated problem by trying to eliminate their reaction to the adversity that is at the heart of the problem. This is sometimes expressed in their goal (e.g., I don't want to feel anxious or have anxious thoughts about 'x'). The reality about human beings is that the more we try to eliminate our experience the more likely it is that we will have this experience, so elimination strategies are in effect problem-maintaining strategies.

Adopting a Façade

Some people are good at adopting a façade or playing a role in situations in which their nominated problem occurs. While this may appear at first sight a good way of dealing with the problem, more considered reflection shows that in playing a role or adopting a façade the person does not deal with the adversity at the heart of the prolthemself. If I play the role of joker in the face of hurtful comments, for example, then I am not dealing constructively with those comments. I am pretending that I am not bothered by them when, in reality, I am.

Seeking Reassurance from Others and from Oneself

When a person is anxious and seeks reassurance from others and/or from oneself, the problem with doing so occurs when that person is not reassurable. This is a feature in anxiety-based problems such as illness anxiety and some forms of obsessive-compulsive related problems. The purpose of reassurance-seeking is for the person to believe that the threat that they fear does not exist or is benign, but this only maintains the problem since the person is not in a state of mind to be convinced by this reassurance. At the core of this issue is often the need for certainty that needs to be addressed if the person is to stop maintaining their problem

Engaging in Unhealthy Behaviours

Another way in which a person unwittingly maintains their nominated problem is to engage in problematic behaviour designed to remove their presently experienced disturbed emotions, but which causes greater problems for them. Take, for example, the use of compulsive behaviour to deal with disturbed feelings with respect to the person's nominated emotional problem. In order to ward off these feelings, the person engages in behaviour that, in the person's mind, has to be done in a certain way, otherwise the person will experience the disturbed feelings. The therapist's task here is twofold: to help the person find a solution to deal with the adversity and let go of the compulsive behaviour so that they can implement the solution.

Complying with Others

When a person has an anxiety-based problem about being disapproved by others and they comply with another person rather than asserting their honestly held view that conflicts with person's view, then the first person can be said to be maintaining their problem. Their compliance not only allows them to avoid the adversity of being disapproved, it reinforces their fear of that adversity. Again the therapist's task is to encourage the client to find a solution to their problem that allows them to face disapproval (in this case) without complying with the other's view.

Being around Others Who Have the Same Problem and Legitimising It

The client's environment can either serve to help that person face their problem or to legitimise it. For example, if the person has a problem with procrastination and lives with others who also leave things to the last minute but do not regard it as a problem, then the client may stop regarding it as a problem. On the other hand, if people in the client's environment do not procrastinate or do procrastinate and regard it as a problem then they may themself regard it as a problem. The effect of the environment needs to be discussed with the client in the search for a solution.

Not Questioning Unhealthy Attitudes and Thinking

Some therapists consider that the client's unhealthy attitudes and thinking have a pivotal role in their problem. For these therapists, the client unwittingly maintains their problems when they do not question these unhealthy attitudes and thinking and allow these cognitive factors sway, unchallenged. For these therapists, helping the client to develop a heathy attitude and associated thinking constitutes an important solution for the client's consideration.

Distracting Oneself from the Problem

Distraction is a major strategy that clients use to focus their attention away from their problem. This clearly serves to maintain their problem by distracting themself, a client learns nothing about dealing constructively with the adversity at the heart of their problem. Once again, the therapist needs to help the person to deal with the adversity so they do not need to distract themself from their problem.

Misusing Substances

A specific way that clients maintain their problem results in them acquiring a second problem that is very frequently more serious than the original problem. This involves the client misusing substances such as food, alcohol, and drugs. These substances are used for several purposes. A person may use them to distract themself from a problem, numb their emotional pain, or substitute feeling good for feeling bad, albeit often only for a short period. As these substances often have an addictive quality, the person becomes dependent in their use (hence the term 'misuse') and the original problem recedes into the background. A person seeking SST may nominate their original problem or their substance misuse problem and it is important to begin with where the client wants to begin. If the person wants to deal with their substance misuse issue, the SST needs to bear in mind that this problem has served, and probably, still serves to protect the person from exposure to the original problem and its effects.

Overcompensating for One's Problem

An example of overcompensation occurs when a person is anxious about a threat and deals with this threat by facing an even greater threat. This is akin to a high jumper who has failed to clear a certain height, raising the bar to an even greater height. When the person fails to deal with the greater threat, they console themselves that this is not surprising and that most people would also fail to deal with it. This manoeuvre serves to maintain the person's problem because they do not face the 'lower level' threat featured in their original problem. It is perhaps unsurprising that when a person uses this problem-maintaining strategy, they are intolerant of what they see as their own weakness in failing to deal with their original problem. The therapeutic task is to encourage the person to face the original, non-overcompensatory threat and if necessary deal with the negative self-judgment that fuels the overcompensation.

Disturbing Oneself for the Presence of the Nominated Problem (Meta-Problem)

The negative self-judgment outlined in the previous section is one example of how a person unwittingly maintains their original problem by disturbing themself about this problem or some feature of it. The technical term for this process is 'meta-problem'.[8] If necessary, and the therapist and client agree to do so, the therapy dyad needs to deal with this meta-problem before addressing the client's original problem.

Knowing the Solution but Waiting for the Presence of Certain Conditions to Implement It

Sometimes a person knows what they need to do to solve their problem, but they don't do it because they are waiting the presence of certain conditions to be present before they take action. For example,

---

8 This literally means having a problem about one's original problem.

a person may say that before they implement the solution, they need to feel comfortable, confident or certain that their solution will work. Given this, they only serve to maintain their problem. The task of the therapist here is to help the client understand that these conditions are desirable rather than necessary and that they can implement the solution in the absence of these conditions.

Giving Up Once the Problem Has Begun Rather than Productively Responding to It

The final problem-maintenance variable that I want to discuss concerns the stance that a person takes to the onset of their problem. If the person responds to the onset of their problem with resignation, then, as they make no attempt to deal with the adversity at the heart of their problem they will unwittingly maintain their problem. The task of the therapist here is to help the person see that the onset of their problem is to be expected but the important point is for them to respond to it constructively.

In what follows, the SST therapist helps the client to identify the major way in which they unwittingly maintain their problem.

SST therapist: So, the problem you want to discuss with me is your anxiety of disapproval by people who you regard as being in authority. Is that right?

Client: Yes

SST therapist: Can you give me an example of this problem either a past example or one you anticipate in the near future?

Client: Yes. Next week we have a meeting with the Head of section and he has a habit of asking people directly for their opinion. I want to give my honest opinion but if you disagree with him he indicates that he disapproves of you.

SST therapist: How does he do that?

Client: He glares at you and turns away sharply and asks someone else for their opinion.

SST therapist: So what's your goal in this meeting?

Client: To not be so scared of his disapproval and to give my honest opinion.

[SST therapist's thinking: Before I help the client with their goal, I want to see how they unwittingly maintain the problem.]

SST therapist: Ordinarily, what would you do in this situation?

Client: Ordinarily, I would try and avoid his eye contact and if he asked me for my opinion, I would basically tell him I agree with him when I don't.

[SST therapist's thinking; The client is using avoidance and compliance so that they don't face disapproval and thus not feel anxious. Let me see if they understand that these are problem-maintenance strategies.]

SST therapist: What do you think of those ways of dealing with the problem?

Client: Not good. They help me in the short term but not in the long term.

SST therapist: So, would you say that they help you to deal with the problem or lead you to maintain the problem unwittingly?

Client: They lead to the maintenance of the problem.

SST therapist: So, would you say that in finding a solution to your problem these strategies have a role or no role?

Client: No role.

[SST therapist's thinking: So, when constructing a solution to the client's problem we can consider drawing on the opposite of these problem-maintenance strategies.]

Chapter 22

Searching for a Solution

Types of Solutions in SST

SST does not favour any one particular solution to the client's nominated problem. As SST is client-led, the therapist encourages the client to choose a solution that the client thinks will be most effective for them. However, it is useful for the therapist to keep in mind that there are several types of solution that they and the client can make use of.

A Reframing Solution

The purpose of a reframing solution is to help the client put an adversity-based problem into a constructive frame so that it is no longer a problem for the person. An example might be a client who is helped to see that their guilt about hurting someone's feelings is evidence that they care about the well-being of that person. What counts here, of course, is whether the person can relate to and is helped by the new frame.

An Attitude Change Solution

An attitude is an evaluative stance that a person takes towards an adversity. From my perspective, when a person has a problem with an adversity, this is likely because the person holds a rigid and extreme attitude towards the adversity. The solution to this issue involves the therapist helping the person develop an alternative flexible and non-extreme attitude towards the same adversity. It is probable that the person will need to practise this new attitude after the session, and as such, the SST therapist needs to help the person to develop the attitude in the session and rehearse it to help the person get an experiential

DOI: 10.4324/9781032657752-26

'feel' of the new attitude and to help the person make an action so that they can implement this new attitude in the future.

An Inference Change Solution

When a client develops an inference about what is happening, they are making a hunch about reality, which may be correct or incorrect. Frequently, the client can never be sure about the validity of their inference and, therefore, they can be encouraged to accept the 'best bet' about what happened, is happening or will happen. Here is an example where a client made an inference change when they could not make an attitude change:

> The SST therapist saw a young man who was very angry about what he described as his mother's intrusiveness, as she would ask him what was on his agenda every time they spoke. His session goal was to not be angry about this. The man insisted that his mother had no right to be intrusive, and all the therapist's efforts to encourage him to be flexible with his attitude fell on deaf ears. Changing tack, the therapist implemented a different strategy designed to help the client examine his inference that her mother was being intrusive. On questioning, the client came to realise that asking people what was on their agenda was just a greeting and not her being intrusive. This strategy proved successful in that the client's anger dissipated because he reinterpreted the meaning behind her 'agenda' question.

A Solution Based on a Change in the Person's Relationship with the Problem

Sometimes an SST therapist can help a client by encouraging a change in their relationship to their problem. This may involve the client seeing what they saw as a problematic response to an adversity as being understandable and one which many people would have made. This helps the client to accept the existence of the response rather than fight against it. Indeed, some SST therapists who practise Acceptance and Commitment Therapy (ACT) reason that a client's struggle with troublesome emotions and dysfunctional thoughts is the problem rather than the emotion and thoughts themselves. When the person stops struggling against these responses, they solve their problem (Bennett & Oliver, 2019).

A Behavioural Change Solution

A solution based on a behaviour change is based on the premise that when a person changes their behaviour, they invite a different response from another person with whom they have a problem. It is important that the therapist takes care in how they introduce this idea since a behavioural change on the part of a client does not guarantee that the other person will respond constructively, but it will increase the chances that this will happen.

In some areas of their life, if a client takes action rather than chooses not to act, then they may improve their situation. For example, when a person chooses to do a task they have been putting off rather than procrastinate on it, it can positively impact their life.

In other areas, it is important that the person refrains from taking action rather than acting in self-defeating ways.

A Situational Change Solution

Occasionally, a client is best served if they change a situation that they are in. For example, a person may be working for a highly demanding manager, and if no other solution is available to help the client, it is probably in their best interest to get a new job.

A Combination of Solutions

While it may be the case that a requires a single solution to their problem (e.g., reframing), for another client a combination of solutions is needed. For example, if a client needs to assert themself with someone, they not only need to change their behaviour but also their attitude in a way that underpins and supports assertive behaviour.

Drawing on a Plethora of Factors in Helping the Client to Select a Solution

In this part of the book, I am working on the assumption that the client has a specific problem that they would like help with. While clients can and do ask for other kinds of help from SST therapists (see Chapter 19), requests for solutions to deal with specific problems are the most frequent form of help sought. Given this, in this section of the book, I will discuss several sources from which therapists can help clients draw. It is important for me to underscore here that nobody is expected to draw upon all these sources with all clients. Think of the following factors as tools in the toolbox of a handyperson. They carry this toolbox around with them not with the expectation that they will use every tool in the box but rather that they will use the tool or tools that are relevant to the situation at hand.

Before discussing the sources from which a client can draw in selecting a solution, I want to stress that unless the client can integrate the implementation of a solution into their everyday life then if the achievement of the client's problem-related goal requires regular practice of that solution, then the therapist should not encourage the client to adopt it.

Different Methods Can Be Used with Different Clients

In my view, SST is a pluralistic way of working with clients. The two main features of pluralism that are relevant here are: i) there is no one absolute right way of understanding clients' problems and their solutions – different viewpoints are useful for different clients, and ii) there is no one absolute right way of practising SST – different clients need different things, and therefore SST therapists need to have a broad practice repertoire.

Drawing on Internal Strengths

SST is a good example of strengths-based therapy (e.g., Jones-Smith, 2014). In SST the therapist searches for the client's strengths in a number of ways.[1] Let me illustrate this in the following example where the therapist is working with a client whose nominated problem is procrastination.

---

1 One of the ways in which the client is asked for the strengths that they can bring to single-session therapy is in the pre-session questionnaire that they are sent once they have made an appointment for SST (see Chapter 15).

SST therapist: So, what strengths do you have as a person that you can bring to the table that would help you address your procrastination problem effectively?

Client: I'm not sure.

SST therapist: Just reflect on the issue for a minute...

Client: No, nothing comes to mind.

[SST therapist thinking: OK, I can either ask the client to tell me what a friend would say about their strengths or what they would say if they were asked the same question about their strengths for a job they really wanted. I think I will go for the latter and keep the former in reserve.]

SST therapist: OK, I want you to imagine that you are being interviewed for a job you really want, and they ask you what strengths as a person do you have that you can bring to the job. How would you answer the question with the proviso that you have to give an honest response?

Client: Good question! I would say that I have determination and once I decide to do something, I will go out of my way to get it done. I would also say that I have compassion for others when they are struggling.

SST therapist: Do you think that you could bring determination and compassion to bear when we figure out a good solution to your procrastination problem?

Client: Yes, I think I could.

Identifying and Using External Resources

There is a phrase that I like to use with clients in single-session therapy. It is 'only you can do it, but you don't have to do it alone'. This means that after the session, the client has the primary responsibility for implementing the solution that they and their therapist have selected, but that they may have recourse to resources external to them that may facilitate the solution-implementation process. For example:

- Other people in the client's environment may be of use in helping them to put the solution into practice.
- The client may get help from organisations that are relevant to the problem at hand.
- Suitable apps and self-help material may supplement the process.

It is the therapist's responsibility not to overload the client with such resources, otherwise, the client will be overwhelmed with information and take away very little from the session. As I discussed in Chapter 10, in SST often 'less is more'.

Using Role Models

A role model in SST is someone that the client respects or looks up to and wishes to emulate in some way. It is important that the gap between the client and the role model to be such that the client believes that they can emulate the person. If the gap between the two is, in the client's mind, too big then the person may think that they won't be able to emulate the role model.

[SST therapist's thinking: I want to see if the client has a role model who can help them with their issue with procrastination. I need to tread carefully here as the choice of a role model is important. I don't want the client to choose someone who does not have a procrastination problem; rather someone who has had an issue with procrastination but has addressed it successfully.]

SST therapist: Do you know anyone who you respect who has effectively addressed a problem with procrastination?

Client: Actually, since you asked, I think that applies to my cousin, Eric.

SST therapist: Do you know how Eric managed that?

Client: Not entirely, but what I do know is that he decided that procrastination was interfering with what was really important to him and that if he did a little bit of work every day and held off on using social media then that would help him... and it did.

SST therapist: What can you take away from Eric's experience that you can use in addressing your issue with procrastination?

Client: Well, I guess I could be clear with myself about the task I am procrastinating on and ask myself if it is important for me to do it. I could set aside a set time every day to do a bit of work on the task, and I could postpone doing tasks that distract me until I have done the work.

SST therapist: Could we add these ingredients to the solution that we are looking for to address your procrastination issue?

Client: For sure.

[SST therapist's thinking: Now let me bring the strengths the client previously mentioned into the mix.]

SST therapist: You mentioned that you could bring your strengths of determination and compassion to the table when addressing your procrastination problem. Are these relevant to what you can take from Eric's example?

Client: Well, certainly determination is.

[SST therapist's thinking: Let me suggest that the client uses imagery to try out these ingredients to see how they feel. I'll put it in a realistic context where the client recognises that they have begun to procrastinate.]

SST therapist: Can I suggest you try these ingredients on for size by me guiding you through an imagery exercise?

Client: OK.

SST therapist: You can do this with your eyes open or closed. Imagine that you have decided that you are going to do a bit of work on the task you have been procrastinating on at a set time. When you sit down to do it, you notice that you are experiencing a tendency to put off doing the task and to engage in social media. Can you imagine this?

Client: [laughing] Easily.

SST therapist: OK. Now see yourself noticing that tendency but responding to it in a determined way by reminding yourself that it is in your interests to do the task for the agreed amount of time and that you are going to do this and can then use social media when you have finished, Can you imagine doing this?

Client: Yes, I can.

SST therapist: How did it feel?

Client: It felt good. I felt a bit awkward at the beginning, but I guess that is to be expected.

SST therapist: It is. What do you think will happen to that awkwardness when you begin the task and stay with it?

Client: It will go.

Using Guiding Principles

We all tend to have what I call guiding principles. These tend to be value-based ideas or attitudes that encourage the person to act in value-based ways in salient aspects of their life. They tend to be pithy, memorable statements that people can bring to mind to help them, for example, deal with adversity. In the context of single-session therapy, they tend to support the implementation of the person's chosen solution. An example from my own life is the phrase, 'If you don't ask, you don't get'. My mother taught me this, and I have used it ever since to push myself forward in order to get something I value. My experiences over the years led me to modify this guiding principle as follows: 'If you don't ask, you don't get. But asking does not guarantee getting'.

The client who sought SST help with his procrastination problem who I presented in the in the above example utilised the following guiding principle in his search for a solution, 'Do, don't stew'. He used this principle when he was thinking about taking action instead of taking action.

Utilising a Client's Prior Helpful and Unhelpful Attempts to Solve the Problem

When people seek help for a problem, it is very likely that they have made a number of attempts to solve the problem. These prior attempts to solve the problem may have been based on the client's intuitive sense of what would be helpful, may have been suggested by other people or the person may have sought therapy before and attempted to implement what they learned from their therapist. Since the person still has the problem, it can be assumed that nothing that the client has tried hitherto has been completely successful. However, it may well be the case that a number have things that the client has tried have yielded *some* benefit to them. The SST therapist's task, therefore, is to assist themself and the client to identify those helping attempts that were helpful to them to some degree and those that were unhelpful to them. The purpose of doing this is to encourage the client to capitalise on those strategies that were useful to them and to cast aside those strategies that were not helpful to them.

SST therapist: Now, you said that have a problem with anger that you would like to address today. How have you tried to deal with your anger issue?

Client: Well, I've tried a few things, but most haven't worked.

SST therapist: What have you tried that hasn't worked?

Client: Techniques to let my anger out like punching cushions and yelling at the cushion as if it were the person I'm angry with. I feel a release when I use these techniques, but they do not help with my anger.

SST therapist: Anything else that hasn't worked?

Client: Relaxation, mindfulness and counting to ten. Again, they calm me down in the moment, but nothing that lasts very long.

[SST therapist's thinking: That's a pretty long list and I don't want the client to become discouraged so let me ask them what has been helpful.]

SST therapist: What have you tried that has been helpful?

Client: Well, nothing has solved the problem but thinking of what the Buddha says helps. You know that phrase, 'Holding on to anger is like grasping a hot coal with the intent of throwing it at someone else; you are the one who gets burned'.

SST therapist: Is it worth building on that while we look for a solution to your anger issue?

Client: Yes, that would be good.

Exceptions: When the Problem Does Not Occur

Ratner, George and Iveson (2012: 106) note that 'It is impossible to behave with total consistency and however stuck in a problem pattern, there will always be exceptions, times when we do something other than the problem, something that with nurturing has the potential to become a solution'. As such, the SST therapist will encourage the client to identify 'exceptions' to their nominated problem – times when the problem does not occur when it might be expected to occur. If an exception can be found, then the therapist works with the client to discover factors which account for the non-occurrence of the problem and then encourage them to use these factors as part of a solution to the problem. Here is an example:

SST therapist: So, every night, you wake up about 2.00 am and go into the kitchen and binge-eat. Is that right?

Client: Yes, that's right.

[SST therapist's thinking. Let's see if there is an exception to this, and if so, let me discover what occasions the exception. I want to find out if the client has ever woken up at 2.00 am and not binged on food, not if she has ever not woken up at 2.00 am. The latter does not tell us that much, the former does.]

SST therapist: Does that happen every night or has there ever been an occasion when you have woken up around 2.00 am and not go into the kitchen to binge on food?

Client: Let me think, No, that does not always happen. Sometimes I wake up and I'm too tired to get up.

[SST therapist's thinking: I could use that example but I am wondering if there is an exception to the problem where the person used psychological factors after waking up to decide not to go into the kitchen to binge-eat.]

SST therapist: OK. Have there been any times when you have woken up at around 2.00 am, weren't too tired to get up to go to the kitchen to binge on food, but decided not to do so?

Client: Yes, there have been a few.

[SST therapist's thinking: Right, now I have a choice. I could ask the client for a specific example on this point, or I could ask them for a theme that, in the client's mind, links these examples. I'm not sure so I will ask the client for guidance.]

SST therapist: I want to help us both understand the factors that helped you not to go into the kitchen to binge-eat on food. From your perspective, is it best to take one example and work that through or to see if there is a theme that links all those occasions, what do you think?

Client: Let's look at one example as I'm not sure there is a theme.

SST therapist: Is there an example that stands out for you?

Client: Yes, one day last week I woke up as usual with the same hungry feeling. However, I remember saying to myself that this feeling is not hunger so it won't be satisfied by food. Then I went back to sleep.

[SST therapist's thinking: I still think that there may be a theme here, so I am going to ask the client for another example.]

SST therapist: That sounds really important in that you considered that you were experiencing a feeling other than hunger and as such, you decided not to go to the kitchen to deal with that feeling with food. Can you recall another example?

Client: Yes, I can, and perhaps there is a theme after all. A few weeks ago, I woke up at 2.00 am as usual, and I remember that the feeling was more defined than usual, and it was loneliness. That's right, I felt lonely. So, I looked at some family photos on

Facebook and that helped me to get back to sleep again without me binge eating.

SST therapist: Do you think that the feeling that you decided wasn't hunger in the first example you mentioned may also have been loneliness?

Client: Now I come to think about it, it could have been.

SST therapist: So, it seems that when you are able to focus on that feeling at 2.00 am in the morning, there may be times when you feel lonely and not hungry, is that right?

Client: I think that if I don't immediately go to the kitchen and ask myself what I am feeling, I think it will be loneliness and not hunger.

SST therapist: Shall we see if we can make use of that insight in the rest of the session today?

Client: Yes. It is important.

Identifying and Utilising Instances of the Client's Goal Occurring

As noted by Ratner et al. (2012), in the development of solution-focused therapy, there was a move away from identifying and working with the client's 'exceptions' to the problem, as discussed above, to identifying and amplifying instances of the client having achieved their goal with respect to their nominated problem. Let me provide an example of how one SST therapist worked with a client to help them identify such an instance.

SST therapist: So you feel scared to upset your mother. What is your goal in relation to this problem?

Client: I want to stand up for what I believe in even if it upsets my mother.

SST therapist: What would you be thinking and feeling while you are doing that?

Client: I would be thinking that I have a right to my view and if my mother gets upset I am sorry about that but I am not responsible for her happiness.

[SST therapist's thinking: I am now going to ask the client if they have ever managed to achieve their goal with their mother.]

SST therapist: Have you ever stood up for what you believe even if it upset your mother because you believed you have a right to your view and that if this upsets your mother that is a shame, but that is not going to stop you?

Client: Yes, once or twice.

[SST therapist's thinking: I want to find out the ingredients that led the client to achieve their goal.]

SST therapist: What was it about these two situations that explains why you were able to achieve your goal?

Client: I think because the subjects were really important to me.

SST therapist: So, you are able to achieve your goal when you think that the subjects are really important for you to be able to do this.

Client: That's interesting. I have not seen it that way. Look I don't want to upset my mother over subjects that don't really matter, but maybe I can speak my mind about all subjects that are important to me. It doesn't only have to be on subjects that are really important to me.

Experiences of Solving the Problem in a Different Area

When a client is in a problem mindset, they tend to forget about times when they may have solved the very problem for which they are currently seeking help, but in a different area of their life. Here, it is the SST therapist's responsibility to discover if this is the case and, if so, to help the client understand this and determine whether the client can transfer this solution to the current nominated problem. Here is an example:

SST therapist: So, what is stopping you from applying for this job since it sounds that you really want it?

Client: I do really want it, but it's the same old story, I don't think I can do it.

SST therapist: So, if you knew you could do the job…?

Client: I would apply for it.

[SST therapist's thinking: This is a good opportunity to see if the client has had the experience of having solved this problem in another area of their life. If so. I can encourage them to transfer this solution to their nominated issue.]

SST therapist: Have you ever had the experience where you thought you could not do something, but you did it and then somewhat later you discovered you could do it?

Client: Let me think. Yes, of course, learning to drive.

SST therapist: Tell me more.

Client: Well, I always wanted to drive a car, and then when my parents bought me driving lessons, I put off booking driving lessons because I thought that I would not be able to drive. However, because I did not want to let my parents down, I booked the lessons, and after a while, I realised that I could drive. Then I passed my test first time.

SST therapist: So, you started off thinking you could not do something, you learned what you thought you could not do and later you discovered you could do it.

Client: I know what you are driving at, if you pardon the pun.

[SST therapist's thinking: I could, of course spell out the point I am making, but it is far better for the client to articulate the point for themselves.]

SST therapist: What am I driving it?

Client: You are saying that I have had the experience of thinking I could not do something, but I did not let that stop me from doing it to see if I could do it.

SST therapist: I could not put that better myself. What do you think of that point?

Client: It's very important.

[SST therapist's thinking: Now I am going to ask the client to transfer the point to the current problem.]

SST therapist: How can you use this learning in the situation where you have been holding off applying for the job you really want?

Client: Well, when I think I can't do the job, I can remind myself that I have thought that before and had been proven wrong. I can apply for the job even if I think I can't do it and discover later whether I can do it or not.

SST therapist: Do they give you on-the-job training?

Client: Yes... I guess that's equivalent to the driving lessons I had.

SST therapist: Good point.

Client: Right, that settles it after the session I am going to prepare my application. Thank you for providing the solution.

[SST therapist's thinking: I could take the credit for that, but it's much better if the client does.]

SST therapist: Don't thank me. Thank your former self who already had the solution. All I did was to reintroduce you to you!

This section and the previous section indicate the following points:

- Clients often do enact instances of their goal.
- They are often not aware of this fact but can use this information when it is pointed out to them.
- Even if a client is aware that they are already meeting their goal, albeit in a different area of their life, they often need help to generalise from one area to the next.

Identifying and Using the Opposite to the Client's Problem-Maintenance Factors

In Chapter 21, I discussed fifteen strategies that clients use to deal with their problems that serve only to maintain these problems. In working with a client, the SST therapist's goal is to help the client to identify the problem-maintaining strategy or strategies that the client employs in order to help them to develop strategies that will help the person to deal with their problem. These strategies will be the opposite of the problem-maintenance strategies (see Table 22.1).

In the example that follows, the client's problem is fear of disapproval from authority figures. The client is discussing an example where he fears speaking his mind with his Head of section, and as shown in Chapter 21, the therapist helped the client to identify their problem-maintenance strategies before using these in the search for a solution to the client's problems.

SST therapist: Ordinarily, what would you do in this situation?

Client: Ordinarily, I would try and avoid his eye contact and if he asked me for my opinion, I would basically tell him I agree with him when I don't.

SST therapist: What do you think of those ways of dealing with the problem?

Client: Not good. They help me in the short term but not in the long term.

SST therapist: So, would you say that they help you to deal with the problem or lead you to maintain the problem unwittingly?

Client: They lead to the maintenance of the problem.

SST therapist: So, would you say that in finding a solution to your problem these strategies have a role or no role?

Client: No role.

[SST therapist's thinking: So, when constructing a solution to the client's problem we can consider drawing on the opposite of these problem-maintenance strategies.]

SST therapist: Let's consider the opposite of what you did in this situation. First, you said that you would avoid eye contact with him. What's the opposite of that?

Client: Making ordinary eye contact with him throughout the meeting.

SST therapist: Then you said that if he asked you for your views during the meeting you would agree with him when actually you hold a different view. What's the opposite of that?

Client: Giving him my honestly held view even if it conflicts with his.

SST therapist: And if you resolved to do both of these things?

Client: I would feel anxious.

[SST therapist's thinking: Here is the tricky bit. I need to help the client see that we need to find a solution to their anxiety problem but that in implementing this solution they need to hold in place the opposite of their problem-maintenance strategies; otherwise, they will neutralise the effects of such a solution.]

SST therapist: Right, so together we will need to find a solution to your anxiety issue. Let's assume that we have found one which you can implement in situations where you are having a meeting with your Head of section. What will happen if while implementing this solution you avoid eye contact with him and continue to agree with his views when you don't agree with him?

Client: I will undermine the solution.

SST therapist: Exactly. We will need to revisit this point later in the session after we have decided upon a solution to your anxiety issue.

Table 22.1 Problem-Maintenance Strategies and Their Opposite

Problem-Maintenance Strategies	Their Opposite
• Avoiding the adversity	• Facing the adversity with the skills to deal with it effectively
• Withdrawing from the adversity	• Staying in the situation where the adversity is present while using skills to deal with it effectively
• Trying to eliminate the adversity or one's reaction to it	• Acknowledging the existence of the adversity and one's reaction to it and dealing with the adversity effectively
• Adopting a façade	• Being oneself and dealing with the adversity effectively without adopting a façade
• Seeking reassurance from others and from self	• Accepting uncertainty related to the adversity
• Engaging in unhealthy behaviours (e.g., compulsions)	• Facing the adversity and dealing with it effectively without engaging in unhealthy behaviours
• Complying with others	• Being oneself and dealing with the adversity effectively without complying with others
• Being around others who have the same problem and legitimising it	• Avoiding others who have the same problem and legitimising it until one has the skills to be with these people and not engage in the problem
• Not questioning unhealthy attitudes and thinking	• Developing healthy attitudes and thinking

Table 22.1 (Continued)

Problem-Maintenance Strategies	Their Opposite
• Distracting oneself from the problem	• Facing and dealing with the adversity central to the person's problem without using distraction
• Misusing substances (food, alcohol, drugs)	• Facing and dealing with the adversity central to the person's problem without using substances
• Overcompensating for one's problem	• Facing and dealing with the adversity central to the person's problem without using overcompensation
• Disturbing oneself for the presence of the nominated problem (meta-problem)	• Undisturbing oneself for the presence of the nominated problem
• Knowing the solution but waiting for the presence of certain conditions to implement it	• Knowing the solution and applying it without waiting for certain conditions to be present
• Giving up once the problematic response has begun rather than productively responding to it	• Accepting the presence of the problematic response and productively responding to it

How the Client and the Therapist View the Solution to the Client's Nominated Problem

In Chapter 21, I discussed the client's view of the problem, the therapist's view of the problem and the importance of them arriving at a shared understanding of the issue. I also discussed the importance of the two identifying the ways in which the client unwittingly maintains the problem. Once an agreed view of the problem's problem has been negotiated, then this should readily suggest a solution to it. This happened in the example I first discussed in Chapter 21, which I will reproduce here.

SST therapist: OK. So, let's go back to your prediction that others will think you are a fool if you say something foolish and let's suppose for the moment that you're correct. OK?

Client: Yes.

SST therapist: Now, it is clear that it is important to you that others don't think you are a fool if you say something foolish. Right?

Client: Right.

SST therapist: Now, which of the following two attitudes leads to your anxiety?

• Attitude 1: 'I don't want others to think that I am a fool if I say something foolish and if they do, they are right. I am a fool' or
• Attitude 2: 'I don't want others to think that I am a fool if I say something foolish and if they do, they are wrong. I am not a fool. I am an ordinary human being which can say foolish and non-foolish things'

Client: The first one leads to my anxiety.

SST therapist: And if you really believed the second attitude, how would you feel about talking in public?

Client: I would feel concerned about them thinking that I would be a fool if I said something foolish, but I wouldn't be anxious about it.

[SST therapist's thinking: I will now ask the client if they want to set concern as a goal with respect to speaking in public and if they do, I can offer Attitude 2 as the solution.]

SST therapist: What do you think of feeling concerned and not anxious with respect to speaking in public as a goal?

Client: I think it is a great idea. I hadn't thought about that before.

SST therapist: And what do you think of developing Attitude 2 as a solution to your problem and as a way of achieving your goal?

Client: I think that if I practised it then it would be a good solution.

SST therapist: Can I show you how to do that?

Client: Yes, please.

After the client has selected a solution, it is important that they give themself the best chance to get the most from it This involves them incorporating the opposite of any of the problem-maintenance strategies they may have used, as shown in the section above.

Chapter 23

Embedding the Solution

Once the therapist and client have agreed on a solution to the client's problem, the next step is for the therapist to help the client to embed the solution. This is particularly important where the solution is attitudinal or cognitive in nature. Just having the awareness that a new attitude, for example, will help the client achieve their problem-related goal is a first step along this process, but the client usually needs a deeper appreciation of the 'healthiness' of the 'to-be-developed' attitude and the unhealthiness of the 'to-be-discarded' attitude. Helping the client to gain such deeper appreciation is an example of what I mean by 'embedding the solution'. The example of this process that I will now present follows on from the dialogue in the example presented above.

> *SST therapist*: And what do you think of developing Attitude 2 as a solution to your problem and as a way of achieving your goal?
>
> *Client*: I think that if I practised it then it would be a good solution.
>
> *SST therapist*: Can I show you how to do that?
>
> *Client*: Yes, please.
>
> *SST therapist*: First, let's remind ourselves of the two attitudes that we looked at:
>
> • Attitude 1: 'I don't want others to think that I am a fool if I say something foolish and if they do, they are right. I am a fool' or

DOI: 10.4324/9781032657752-27

- Attitude 2: 'I don't want others to think that I am a fool if I say something foolish and if they do, they are wrong. I am not a fool. I am an ordinary human being which can say foolish and non-foolish things'

[SST therapist's thinking: I will now need to explain what I plan to do and get the client's permission to proceed.]

SST therapist: I am going to ask you some questions about both attitudes and then you have a more informed view of which attitude you wish to develop, and which attitude you wish to discard. Is that OK?

Client: That's fine.

The therapist then proceeded to ask the client questions designed to help them examine both attitudes and choose which one they wanted to develop based on a deeper appreciation of the truth, logic and healthiness of Attitude 2 and the false nature, illogic and unhealthiness of Attitude 1.

When the work that the client and therapist do in this solution-embedding process is based largely on the therapist's view of the problem and its solution, the client does not have a view on such matters and is looking to the therapist to provide one. Consequently, this work is influenced by the ideas associated with the therapist's therapeutic orientation preferences. So, for example, the work that the therapist and client did in the example presented above was influenced by the therapist's allegiance to Rational Emotive Behaviour Therapy (see Dryden, 2024a). However, it is important to note that on other occasions, the solution-embedding process is based on a solution created by both client and therapist and draws on the factors discussed earlier in this chapter. Here, the imprint of the therapist's therapeutic allegiances will be less pronounced or, indeed, absent.

Chapter 24

Encouraging the Client to Rehearse the Solution

If you want to buy a new car, you will probably want to take it for a test drive in order to judge how it 'feels' to drive the car. You might like the look of it, but if you don't feel comfortable behind the wheel, then you won't buy it. This is also the case when you have helped your client to select a solution. Before you discuss with them how they can best implement this solution, suggest that they rehearse it. The purpose of such rehearsal is twofold:

- First, it is to help the client to determine whether they can fully commit to implementing the solution. If not, the therapist needs to help them to judge whether some tweaks can be made to the solution so that they can fully commit to it or whether a new solution should be sought.
- Second, if the client is sure that they can commit to implementing their chosen solution, rehearsing it is a prelude to action.

Methods of Rehearsing the Solution

There are a number of ways in which a client can rehearse their selected solution. I will discuss three here: i) roleplay; ii) imagery and iii) chairwork.

Roleplay

Roleplay rehearsal can be used when a client wants to say something to another person and needs to practise this. Here the therapist plays the role of the other person and thus needs to be briefed by the client concerning what the other person is like and how they are likely to respond to the client. It is likely that as part of the solution the client

DOI: 10.4324/9781032657752-28

was helped by the therapist to develop a certain state of mind which enables them to say what they need to say to the other person. Before the roleplay, the therapist can suggest to the client that they first enter that state of mind before engaging in the behavioural roleplay.

What follows is an example of roleplay with a client whose problem is that she wants to spend some time with her friends, but does not assert herself with her mother for fear of upsetting her. Her goal is to assert herself with her mother without feeling guilty. The state of mind that she has chosen to develop to help her do this is, 'I have a right to spend some time with my friends and I am not going to buy my mother's propaganda that I don't care about her and that I am a bad daughter. I do care, I am a good daughter, but I need time with my friends.' Before the roleplay, the client briefed the therapist with respect to her mother's likely responses. She also got herself into the state of mind outlined above. The client and therapist have agreed that the therapist will give the client ongoing feedback about her assertive efforts.

Client: Mother, Stephanie and Ruth have asked me out for dinner on Friday evening, is it alright if I go?[1]

[SST therapist's thinking: The client is asking for her mother's opinion, rather than telling her mother what she is going to do. I will need to bring this to the client's attention.]

SST therapist: Let me interrupt you. By asking that question, what are you doing?

Client: I am asking for her permission.

SST therapist: Do you want to do that?

Client: No.

SST therapist: What can you say instead?

Client: I can inform her of my plans without asking for her permission.

SST therapist: OK let's go back to the roleplay. Just begin again.

---

1 The roleplay sections are underlined.

Client: Mother, Stephanie and Ruth have asked me out for dinner on Friday evening, so I intend to go.

SST therapist (as mother): That's nice dear, but what about me? I'll be all on my own.

Client: You have lots of friends you can ask round.

SST therapist (as mother): I don't want to ask anyone round. I enjoy our Friday evenings together. Don't leave me on my own.

Client: If you want to be on your own that is your choice, but I am going out for dinner with my friends.

SST therapist (as mother): That's right, put yourself first as always. You don't care about how I feel.

Client: Mother that's really unfair. I rarely put myself first and how can you say I don't care about me?

[SST therapist's thinking: The client is trying to persuade her mother that she rarely puts herself first and that she does care. She doesn't realise that she is being manipulated here. I need to bring this to her attention.]

SST therapist: Let me interrupt you. What's the purpose of what you have just said to your mother?

Client: I am trying to persuade her that I care and I'm not selfish.

SST therapist: Is that likely to be successful?

Client: No.

SST therapist: Why not?

Client: Because my mother is trying to manipulate me through guilt as she always does.

SST therapist: So, what are your options at this point?

Client: To persuade her that I care and am not selfish or to reiterate my plans.

SST therapist: What's in your healthy interests to do?

Client: To reiterate my plans.

SST therapist: OK let's go back to the roleplay. I'll feed you your mother's line again.

SST therapist (as mother): That's right, put yourself first as always. You don't care about how I feel.

Client: Mother, I am not getting involved in this, I am letting you know my plans. You can decide what you want to do on Friday night.

SST therapist (as mother): You're not a good daughter are you?

Client: Mother, I'll see you later. I am going up to my room to write up some reports.

SST therapist: How did that feel?

Client: A mixture of good and bad. I was pleased I was able to express my view and not get involved in my mother's manipulative ploys, but I also feel bad if she feels bad.

SST therapist: That is understandable. But you can feel bad that your mother is feeling bad but still go out with your friends, or you can feel bad if you don't go out with them because you are not living your own life.

Client: Yes, I see. There is no alternative to feeling bad. The important thing is what I choose to do.

The therapist and client then roleplayed the situation again at the end of which, the client committed herself to assert herself with her mother in the manner outlined above that evening.

Imagery

The use of imagery methods in SST is largely as described at the beginning of this chapter: to give the client an opportunity to get an experience of what it feels like to enact the solution or to get mental practice at implementing the solution to which the client has already committed themselves. Here is an example of the latter with the client discussed above. The therapist uses guided imagery, guiding the client through the solution that they developed in the session and refined through roleplay. You will note that the therapist introduces the idea that the client is struggling at various points. I consider that this is an important point. In all probability, clients will initially struggle to implement solutions and it is best to reflect such realism in the imagery method than to suggest that they can implement the solution with ease. The latter is unlikely, certainly at the outset.

[SST therapist's thinking: My plan is to use guided imagery where I take the client step-by-step through the solution that we have refined and then have her do this mental rehearsal without any guidance from me.]

SST therapist: So, we have agreed that it would be good for you to mentally rehearse asserting yourself with your mother. Let me take you through a guided imagery which incorporates the main points that we have discussed so far and then you can practise this on your own without any help from me. OK?

Client: That's fine.

SST therapist: You can do this with your eyes closed or eyes open. See yourself first getting yourself into the following state of mind, 'I have a right to spend some time with my friends and I am not going to buy my mother's propaganda that I don't care about her and that I am a bad daughter. I do care, I am a good daughter, but I need time with my friends.' Then see yourself with that state of mind in place going to see your mother to tell her of your plans for Friday evening. Notice that you feel uncomfortable about doing this but determined to do so.

See yourself telling your mother that you are going out for dinner with your friends on Friday evening and that she can invite some of her friends round if she wants to. Imagine that your mother accuses you of being selfish and uncaring, and while you feel the urge to respond, you remind yourself that this is her attempt to manipulate you, and you don't do so. You reiterate your plans and leave the room after she accuses you of being a bad daughter. You are sad about her accusation, but you know it is not true and you feel good about asserting yourself and that you have not fallen for your mother's guilt-inducing strategy.

How does that feel?

Client: It feels good. I can see that I can assert myself even if I feel bad about what my mother said.

SST therapist: OK, now I'll stay silent and you can guide yourself through this scenario in your mind's eye.

Chairwork

Chairwork involves the client having a dialogue with different parts of themselves or with another person using chairs to represent these different aspects. The role of the SST therapist while using chairwork with a client is to keep in mind the solution that the client is trying to develop and to keep the focus on the client developing this. In my view, for the therapist to use chairwork in SST, it is best for the therapist to have had some prior training in and experience of using this method in therapy (see Pugh, 2019).[2]

---

2 Pugh (2021) has developed a chairwork-based approach to SST which does require training in both SST and chairwork.

Chapter 25

Helping the Client to Develop and Implement an Action Plan

As I pointed out in Chapter 22, there are solutions which don't need to be acted upon. These solutions tend to involve clients being helped to see things from a different perspective, and when this is done, it does not need to be practised. However, most solutions, particularly those which involve clients changing habitual behaviour, do require the client to practise the solution over time. When this is the case, it is important for the therapist to help the client to develop an action plan for them to implement. Wikipedia defines an action plan as 'a detailed plan outlining actions needed to reach one or more goals. Alternatively, it can be defined as a sequence of steps that must be taken, or activities that must be performed well, for a strategy to succeed'.[1]

Action Plans vs. Homework Assignments

An action plan differs from homework assignments. In ongoing therapy[2] where homework is a regular feature of the work, the therapist negotiates a homework assignment with a client at the end of the session with the expectation that the client will carry out the assignment in the period between the end of the current session and the beginning of the next one. The assignment ideally should be specific and should reflect the work done in the session that is about to end and should involve the client in doing something constructive or refraining from doing something unconstructive. This behavioural task is often

---

1 https://en.wikipedia.org/wiki/Action_plan
2 There are, of course, many approaches to therapy where the negotiating and reviewing of homework assignments do not feature.

DOI: 10.4324/9781032657752-29

accompanied by the rehearsal of a healthy attitude or constructive way of thinking. As part of the negotiation process, the therapist ensures that the client understands the task, sees the connection between carrying out the task and the goal that they have set for therapy and helps the client to identify any obstacles to task completion and if these are mentioned, encourages them to deal effectively with the obstacles so that they are free to do the negotiated task. At the beginning of the following session, the therapist reviews with the client their experiences in doing the assignment.

There are two main differences between an action plan and a homework assignment. First, an action plan tends to be more general than a homework assignment since it will need to be implemented across situations. Second, if a client only attends for a single session in SST and does not seek further help then there is no opportunity for the therapist to review how they got on with implementing the plan. However, there are similarities between the two. Both stem from the session that took place and obstacles to implementing both the action plan and homework assignments are identified and a plan put in place to deal with these obstacles.

Elements of a Good Action Plan

In most instances in single-session therapy, it should be remembered that results are achieved by the client outside the session and that the achievement of the client's session goal represents the beginning of a process of change rather than the end of it – namely, when the client has reached their problem-related goal. Having made this point, let me discuss several features of a good action plan that should be considered by both client and therapist as they work together to draw up such a plan.

Client Responsibility

The client needs to take responsibility for implementing the plan. If the client is not prepared to take ownership of implementing the action plan, then there is no point in the therapist helping them to develop the plan. Thus, before such work is undertaken the therapist should ascertain that the client is prepared to do whatever they agree should be a part of the action plan.

Integrating the Solution into the Client's Life

The client should be able to integrate the plan into their life. If they are not able to do this, they may begin to initiate the plan but quickly stop doing so because of the effort required is, in their mind too great. I am not suggesting here that the client should only implement an action when it is easy for them to do so. What I am saying is that when it is part of the client's everyday routine, then they are more likely to implement the plan over time than when it is not part of their schedule. For example, it is not easy for a person with diabetes to inject themself with insulin several times a day but if they make it part of their every routine then they will be able to maintain doing so.

The Importance of Clarity

What the client has agreed to do needs to be clear. Therefore, the more specific the solution delineated in the action plan, the better.

Remembering the Purpose of the Solution

The client needs to see clearly how implementing the action plan can lead to the achievement of their problem-related goal. It will also help if the client keep this connection at the forefront of their mind when implementing the solution in their everyday life (see below).

The Components of a Good Solution

Perhaps the most important part of a solution-focused action plan is its components. These components are as follows:

- *What* the client has agreed to do (i.e., the aspects of the solution).
- *Why* the client has agreed to implement the solution.
- *When* the client has agreed to implement the solution.
- *Where* the solution is to be implemented.
- *Who* the solution is to be implemented with.
- *How often* is the solution to be implemented.

Strengths

In Chapter 22, I discussed that the SST therapist works to identify the client's strengths or inner resources so that the client can bring the most relevant of these to salient aspects of the SST process. This is certainly the case when the therapist is helping the client to develop an action plan. In particular, the strengths of determination and persistence are particularly valuable with developing and implementing an action plan.

Support

I also mentioned in Chapter 22 that other people in the client's life can be helpful to them during the SST process. Here, it is important for the therapist to help the client to nominate those who can help them initiate an action plan and sustain it over the long term.

Identifying and Dealing with Anticipated Obstacles

It is very useful for the therapist to help the client to identify potential obstacles to them implementing the action plan so that they can think about how they would respond should they encounter each obstacle.

Monitoring

It is important for the therapist to encourage the client to establish some kind of monitoring system that they can use to track their progress at implementing the solution. This can serve both to encourage the client and to identify unanticipated obstacles which they can then deal with once they have been recognised.

In the following example, I will demonstrate how one therapist used some of the above points while helping the client to develop an action plan.

SST therapist: So, let's be clear what your solution is.

Client: It is to assert myself with my mother when she tries to manipulate me with guilt when I want to go out and spend time with my friends. Before I do this, I will remind myself that I am a good daughter and I have a right to spend time with my friends.

SST therapist: And what is the purpose of doing this?

Client: To have a life independent of my mother and not feel guilty about it.

[SST therapist's thinking: So we know the 'what', the 'why' and the 'who with', now let me find out about the 'where', the 'when' and the 'frequency'.]

SST therapist: When are you going to implement this solution?

Client: Every time I want to go out with my friends and my mother tries to stop me.

[SST therapist's thinking: That takes care of the 'when', the 'where' and the 'frequency', now let's see what strengths the client can bring to the table and who can support them in their journey towards their goal.]

SST therapist: Which of your strengths that we discussed earlier do you think that you can use to help you to implement this solution going forward?

Client: My determination to be independent of my mother and live a life of my own.

SST therapist: Excellent. Is there anyone in your circle who can support you as you implement your action plan?

Client: My friend Sarah. She is a real encouragement to me without nagging me as some of my other friends would do.

SST therapist: So will you ask Sarah for her encouragement?

Client: Yes.

[SST therapist's thinking: The client seems very determined to put her solution into practice but let's see if she can anticipate any obstacles to her implementation this action plan.]

SST therapist: You seem very determined to action your solution and that's great. I'm wondering if you can foresee any obstacles that might prevent you from doing so?

Client: Yes. If my mother says that she is ill when I tell her I am going out with my friends, I will struggle to leave her under those conditions.

[SST therapist's thinking. I need to help her to distinguish between real illness and feigned illness here. If her mother really is ill then the client can't be expected to leave her but she may well feign illness as another manipulative ploy.]

SST therapist: Does your mother generally tell you if she is ill?

Client: Yes, she does.

SST therapist: And if she is genuinely ill, does she wait to tell you until you inform her that you are going out with your friends?

Client: That is an excellent point. No, if she is genuinely ill, she would tell me straight away rather than wait until I tell her I am going out. So, do you think she would feign illness to stop me from going out?

SST therapist: What do you think?

Client: Yes, my mother would do this. I need to remember that when I tell my mother that I am going out with my friends and she responds by telling me she is ill I know she is feigning illness. I will respond sympathetically but will be firm in my resolve to go out.

SST therapist: Any other obstacle?

Client: Not that I can think of.

[SST therapist's thinking: Finally, I need to ask the client how she will monitor her progress.]

SST therapist: How will you monitor your progress in implementing your action plan?

Client: I will keep a notebook and write down every time my mother tried to stop me from going out and how I responded.

SST therapist: Excellent. And if there is any occasion when you failed to assert yourself, what will you do?

Client: I will figure out how I stopped myself from doing so and see if I can learn from that experience.

The Action Plan and Achievement vs. Maintenance of the Client's Problem-Related Goal

While the purpose of the action plan is to help the client to achieve their problem-related goal, once this target has been met, the client will need to maintain their progress. In some ways, maintaining a goal is perhaps more difficult than achieving it in the first place. If the client does struggle to maintain their goal, then they should know that they can return for another single session to get some help with maintaining their gains.

Chapter 26

Ending the Session

Once the therapist has helped the client to develop an action plan which they will implement after the session, then this is a marker that the session is drawing to a close. It is important that the therapist and client end the session on a positive note. Jerome Frank (1961) made the point that while people who seek therapeutic help come with a myriad of different symptoms, what tends to unite them is that they are in a state of demoralisation. If the therapist can help the client leave with the sense of their morale restored, then this, in my view, is a positive outcome from the session. What I will discuss now are ways of ending the session that promote a good ending and help the client leave the session in a hopeful state of mind.

Asking the Client for a Session Summary

The first thing that an SST therapist tends to do when the session is coming to a close is to ask the client to summarise the work that the two of them have done in the session. One might think that it is the job of the therapist to put forward a summary of what the two have covered in the session, but this is not the case for two reasons. First, asking the client to summarise the work keeps the client in an active state of mind which is important throughout the SST process. If the therapist were to provide a summary of the session, then this would tend to render the client passive, which is to be avoided if possible. Second, it is important that the client takes away from the session what *they* consider to be the main points that the two of them discussed in the session. The client's summary will highlight these main points. If the therapist provides a session summary, then this would reflect what the *therapist* considers to be the main points discussed.

DOI: 10.4324/9781032657752-30

When the client provides the session summary, this does not mean that the therapist is forbidden from adding to it. Far from it, it may be that the client's summary omits a salient point. If so, the therapist would offer it as something that the client *could* add to their summary and not what they *should* add to it. Ideally, the client's summary should include the main points discussed, the solution decided upon and how this solution is to be implemented.

Asking for Takeaways

A takeaway in SST literally represents what a client is going to take away from the session that is meaningful and that will, in the client's view, make a difference to their life after the session. A takeaway should include the solution that the therapist and client have agreed on and that features significantly in the action plan that the two have developed to help the client to implement the solution. However, a takeaway may also include other points with which the client resonated with during the session.

The therapist should ideally ask the client for their takeaways after the latter has provided their session summary. If the takeaway does not include the solution this would warrant discussion between the therapist and client as it *may* cast doubt on the relevance of the solution that the client has selected.

It is useful for the therapist to ask the client to make a note of both their agreed solution and their takeaways from the session.

Helping the Client to Generalise the Solution/ Takeaways

Another important task that the therapist has towards the end of the session is to explore with the client whether they can generalise their takeaways and/or the chosen solution to similar instances of the same problem and also to different problems. If a client can see ways of generalising their learning then this increases the therapeutic potency of SST.

Exploring Future Help Options

Before ending it is vital that the therapist reviews with the client what their options are concerning access further help. These options need to be put forward with equal emphasis and that whichever option the client chooses is OK. The possible options are as follows:

- *To decide not to seek further help for the time being.*

This may because the client has achieved what they have come for or that they have not been helped. The client is informed that they can seek further help in the future if they wish.

- *To implement the chosen solution and takeaways and see what happens.*

The client engages in a process of reflecting on what they got from the session, digesting it to see how it relates to other areas of their life, taking action, letting time pass before deciding whether or not to seek further help. As discussed in the final part of the book, some agencies impose a waiting period on clients by telling them that they will receive a call from the agency designed to see how they are getting on and whether or not they want more help.

- *To seek further help at the end of the session.*[1]

From a single-session perspective if a client wants to access further help at the end of the session they should be given a clear indication of what help is available from the independent practitioner (with any costs involved) of from the agency in which they have been seen. They should ideally be given accurate information about the waiting times that are current to access the various services on offer. If they require specialist help that the practitioner or agency cannot provide, then a referral should be made to a service that does provide such help and if this cannot be done then this should be made clear to the client.

Asking for Last-Minute Questions and Statements

Before the session is brought to a close, it is useful if the therapist covers two areas briefly so that the session can come to a satisfactory end. It sometimes happens that SST clients regret not saying something or asking something when they get home. To prevent this from happening, the therapist can ask the following questions:

---

1 As has been mentioned several times before, there are those in the SST community who would not conclude this as an option. For these therapists, an integral part of SST is giving the client the time to reflect on, digest and implement their chosen solution and other takeaways. Then, these therapists argue, the client is best placed to decide whether or not to request further help.

- Is there anything you wish to ask about the issue we have discussed today that you may have wished you had asked when you get home?
- Is there anything you wish to say about the issue we have discussed today that you may have wished you had said when you get home?

It is important that the therapist discourages the client from raising a different issue in response to these questions.

What follows is an example of how a therapist ended an SST session with a client demonstrating some of the issues discussed above.

SST therapist: As we are approaching the end of the session, I wonder if you would summarise what we discussed today?

Client: OK. We discussed my difficulty asserting myself with my mother because I feel guilty about upsetting her. We decided that what I need to do is to stand up for myself with my mother when she tries to guilt-trip me when I want to go out with my friends. To prepare myself for this, I will remind myself that I am a good daughter and I have a right to spend time with my friends. We outlined an action plan to help me to put this solution into practice.

[SST therapist's thinking: That is an excellent summary. Let's see what the client's takeaways are.]

SST therapist: Aside from this, what are you going to take away from the session?

Client: That I am entitled to my own life and as long as I don't needlessly harm my mother, I am going to get that life.

SST therapist: Can you see ways in which you can generalise the solution and that takeaway to other areas of your life?

Client: Yes, I need to assert myself at work. People assume that I will do more than I am supposed to because I have let them think that because I always say 'yes' to everything. I am going to start saying 'no' and let people deal with their own disappointment.

[SST therapist's thinking: The client seems to have got a lot from the session, I wonder if she will opt for more help or not. Let's see.]

SST therapist: Excellent. Let me outline what your options are going forward. OK?

Client: Fine.

SST therapist: All these options are from my perspective, perfectly fine.

First, you could decide that you have got the help that you have come for and don't need any more help at this time. If you decide on this option you can always seek help at some future date.

Second, you could decide to put what you have learned into practice and see how that goes and then make a decision if you need more help.

Third, you could decide now that you would like further help in which case we would review what's available and how long you would have to wait for each service.[2]

Which option would you like to select?

Client: The first one. I have certainly got what I came for and am looking forward to putting it into practice. But it's good to know I can come back.

[SST therapist's thinking: OK, I will now give the client a chance to ask me anything or tell me anything before we wrap things up.]

SST therapist: Have you got anything to ask me about the issue we have discussed or tell me about the issue that you may have wished you had asked or told me when you get home?

Client: No, I'm good to go.

---

2 Again, this option would be omitted by certain SST therapists.

Afterword
After the Session

Preamble

There is a minority view in the single-session therapy community that says that SST should only include the session itself – no contact between the client and therapist or agency before the session takes place and no follow-up after the session. However, most people in the SST community do not concur with this view saying that both pre-session contact and follow-up should be seen as part of the SST process (Hoyt, 2018).

I am agreement with the latter viewpoint and consider that there are three points of contact that need to be considered after the session has finished: i) seeking immediate feedback; ii) checking-in and iii) longer term evaluative feedback.

After the Session

In the current therapeutic climate, gaining immediate client feedback, checking in with the client and carrying out a longer-term follow-up evaluation with the client are de rigueur. So let me briefly discuss each in turn and give an example of each.

Seeking Immediate Client Feedback

Since the SST therapist may never see their client again, it is instructive to understand what the client made of their session with the therapist. In my own work for an online therapy agency where the modal number of sessions clients have is '1', I ask my client at the end of their session with me if they would complete a brief feedback form

DOI: 10.4324/9781032657752-31

so that I know how helpful the session has been for them. Once they agree, I send them a form to complete and return (see Appendix 2).

In an ideal world, the client would send the feedback form to someone other than the therapist since it is difficult to be critical of the therapist if the client knows that the therapist will read the form.

This form can be very useful for an agency offering single-session therapy as it will help the agency monitor the experiences of clients who see different therapists. This will help the agency to identify therapists who are not seen as helpful by clients and thus prompt remedial action on behalf of the agency.

Checking-In with the Client

As I discussed in Chapter 26, some agencies that offer SST contact clients, usually by phone, to check-in with them after the session, see how they are doing and to ask if they need more help. This is usually done two or three weeks after the session. An example of such a check-in comes from the Bouverie Centre, a family therapy centre in Melbourne, Australia famous for its SST work. They say the following:

> During the follow-up phone call, the worker seeks feedback about the session, provides further assistance, if appropriate, and makes a collaborative decision with the client about what further action (if any) is needed. Options include all available services: a second single session, ongoing work, referral to another program within the service, referral to another service or no action (usually with an invitation to re-contact, if necessary, in the future).

This is very similar to the options offered to the client at the end of the session as described in Chapter 26 with one major difference, agencies like the Bouverie Centre do not give clients the opportunity routinely to seek help at the end of the session.

Seeking Longer-Term Evaluative Follow-Up

By longer-term follow-up, I mean contact with a client two or more months after the final contact with the contact to find out what difference the session(s) made to their life and what they thought of the service that they were offered.

Such follow-up also provides the client with an opportunity to tell the therapist or agency representative what they have done since the final contact. In my experience, many clients appreciate such an opportunity.

From the therapist's or agency's perspective longer-term follow-up provides them outcome evaluation data (i.e., how the client has done). These data can help improve the therapeutic delivery of SST services.

Finally, longer-term follow-up provides the agency which offers SST with service evaluation data (i.e., the client's experience of seeking help from the agency). Such data can help the agency improve the organisational delivery of SST services.

My Approach to Follow-Up

Here, I will discuss the situation where I conduct a longer-term follow-up with a client who has decided that they got what they wanted from their first and only session of ONEplus therapy.[1]

My preference is to carry out the follow-up appointment by telephone. This is to make it distinct from the online ONEplus therapy session and have it interactive. For this reason, I prefer not to use a questionnaire for follow-up purposes. I have presented my follow-up telephone protocol in Appendix 3. Please note that I choose not to use objective forms to measure outcomes. I do realise, however, that many SST therapists employ such measures, and if these are used, these measures need to be given to the client to complete pre-session and at follow-up.

We have now reached the end of the book. I hope you have found it useful. Any feedback that you have to offer please send to me at windy@windydryden.com

---

1 If you recall, I refer to my approach to SST as ONEplus therapy.

Appendix 1

Therapeutic Contract with Professor Windy Dryden

ONEplus Therapy

Here are the elements of my practice that you need to know and agree with before you become a client of mine. This document should be read in conjunction with the accompanying leaflet on ONEplus therapy[1] that outlines its nature.

About me: I have had almost 50-years-experience working with clients as a psychotherapist. I have had over 1,000 hours experience practising ONEplus therapy. I offer other forms of therapy delivery as outlined on my website (www.windydryden.com). Please familiarise yourself with this information before deciding that you wish to access ONEplus therapy.

1   We will meet either face-to-face or online by Zoom.
2   If we are meeting online by Zoom, I will send you a link in advance.
3   All our meetings are confidential with the exception of the following:

   a   If you are at risk to yourself and are not prepared to take steps to protect your life or well-being, I will take steps to protect you in these respects.

   b   If you pose a risk to others and are not prepared to take steps to protect them, then I will take steps to protect them from you.

   c   I am professionally mandated to report past or present incidents of child abuse that have not previously been reported.

---

1 See Chapter 12 for the leaflet on ONEplus therapy that I send to prospective clients.

d   If I am formally requested to hand over my notes to the courts then I am obliged to do so.

4   I will not speak or correspond with others about you without your formal, written permission. If anybody contacts me about you and I do not have your written authority to speak or correspond with them, then I will not do so and will inform you about this.

5   I have a 48-hour cancellation policy. This means that I will charge you if you do not give me full 48-hour notice that you wish to cancel your appointment. If I do not give you full 48-hour notice if I need to cancel our appointment, then you do not pay for your next session. The exception to this is if either you, I or one of our loved ones have to be hospitalised.

6   Before the session, I will send you a pre-session questionnaire for you to complete and return. The main purpose of the form is to help you to get the most from the session.

7   My fee is £__ per session (up to 50-minute session) payable by BACS at the end of the session. This includes my processing of your pre-session questionnaire, the session and the audio-recording of the session.

8   If you want a transcript of the session this will be £__ extra. Please tell me whether or not you want this transcript.

9   If we agree a follow-up appointment there will be an extra charge depending on what type of follow-up we decide to have.

10 My BACS details are as follows:

Please confirm that you agree with these conditions by signing and dating a copy of this form and returning it to me. If you have any questions about ONEplus therapy or the terms of this contract that you want answered before you give your informed consent to proceed, please email them to me. Only sign the contract when your questions have been answered to your satisfaction.

I have read the above and agree with the conditions stated. I have also read the leaflet on ONEplus therapy that I have been sent. I further attest that I am seeking ONEplus therapy voluntarily.

Signed.....................................

Date..

ONEplus Therapy Session Rating Scale

Name: Date:

It is very important for me to monitor my counselling work. So, please rate the session you recently had with me by UNDERLINING the number that best fits your experience on the following scales.

The pre-session questionnaire was not useful in helping me to prepare for the session	0 1 2 3 4 5 6 7 8 9 10	The pre-session questionnaire was useful in helping me to prepare for the session
I did not feel heard, understood or respected by Windy Dryden in the session	0 1 2 3 4 5 6 7 8 9 10	I did feel heard, understood and respected by Windy Dryden in the session
Windy Dryden and I did not discuss what I I wanted to discuss in the session	0 1 2 3 4 5 6 7 8 9 10	Windy Dryden and I did discuss what I wanted to discuss in the session
Windy Dryden's approach was not for me good fit for me	0 1 2 3 4 5 6 7 8 9 10	Windy Dryden's approach was a good fit for me

Overall, I did not get what I wanted from my session with Windy Dryden	0 1 2 3 4 5 6 7 8 9 10	Overall, I did get what I wanted from my session with Windy Dryden
If I wanted another counselling session, I would not choose Windy Dryden as my counsellor	0 1 2 3 4 5 6 7 8 9 10	If I wanted another counselling session, I would choose Windy Dryden as my counsellor

Finally, if there was anything that was particularly useful or anything I could have done to have improved the session for you, please let me know in the box below:

Thank you for your feedback. Please email this form back to _____

Follow-Up Telephone Evaluation Protocol

1   Check that the client has the time to talk now (i.e., approximately 20–30 minutes)? Are they able and willing to talk freely, privately and in confidence?

Client Response:

2   Read to the client verbatim their original statement of the problem, issue, obstacle or complaint. Ask: 'Do you recall that?', 'Is that accurate?'

Client Response:

3   Would you say that the issue (re-state as described by the client) is about the same or has changed? If changed, list five-point scale as follows:

(1)-------------(2)-------------(3)-------------(4)-------------(5)
Much worse   About the same   Much improved

Client Response:

4   What do you think made the change (for better or worse) possible.
    If conditions are the same, ask 'What makes it stay the same?'

    Client Response:

5   If people around you give you the feedback that you have
    changed, how do they think you have changed?

    Client Response:

6   Besides the specific issue of... (state the problem), have there been
    other areas that have changed (for better or worse). If so what?

    Client Response:

7   Now please let me ask you a few questions about the therapy that
    you received. What do you recall from that session?

    Client Response:

8   What do you recall that was particularly helpful or unhelpful?

    Client Response:

9 How have you been able to make use of the session recording if at all? If so, what was helpful about it?

Client Response:

10 If you received a written transcript of the session, what use did you make of it?

Client Response:

11 How satisfied are you with the therapy that you received? Ask the client to make their rating on the five-point scale as follows and ask them to explain their rating:

(1)--------------(2)--------------(3)--------------(4)--------------(5)
Very   Neither Satisfied   Very
Dissatisfied   Nor Dissatisfied   Satisfied

Client Response:

12 Did you find the single session to be sufficient? If not, would you wish to resume therapy? Would you wish to change therapist?

Client Response:

13 If you had any recommendations for improvement in the service
    that you received, what would they be?

    Client Response:

14 Is there anything else I have not specifically asked you that you
    would like me to know?

    Client Response:

Thank the client for their time and participation. Remind them that
they can contact you or the agency again if they need further help.

References

Barnett, J. E. (2015, March). Informed consent in clinical practice: The basics and beyond. Retrieved from www.societyforpsychotherapy.org/informed-consent-in-clinical-practice-the-basics-and-beyond

Bennett, R., & Oliver, J. E. (2019). *Acceptance and Commitment Therapy: 100 Key Points and Techniques*. Abingdon: Routledge.

Bion, W. R. (1967). Notes on memory and desire. *Psychoanalytic Forum, 2*, 272–273.

Bordin, E. S. (1979). The generalizability of the psychoanalytic concept of the working alliance. *Psychotherapy: Theory, Research and Practice, 16*, 252–260.

Brown, G. S., & Jones, E. R. (2005). Implementing a feedback system in a managed care environment: What are patients teaching us? *Journal of Clinical Psychology, 61*, 187–198.

Campbell, L. F., Norcross, J. C., Vasquez, M. J., & Kaslow, N. J. (2013). Recognition of psychotherapy effectiveness: the APA resolution. *Psychotherapy, 50* (1), 98–101.

Cannistrà, F. (2022). The single session therapy mindset: Fourteen principles gained through an analysis of the literature. *International Journal of Brief Therapy and Family Science, 12* (1), 1–26.

Cooper, M., & Law, D. (2018). (Eds.), *Working with Goals in Counselling and Psychotherapy*. Oxford: Oxford University Press.

Dryden, W. (2011). *Counselling in a Nutshell*. 2nd edition. London: Sage.

Dryden, W. (2017). *Single-Session Integrated CBT (SSI-CBT): Distinctive Features*. Abingdon: Routledge.

Dryden, W. (2018). *Very Brief Therapeutic Conversations*. Abingdon: Routledge.

Dryden, W. (2020). *The Single-Session Counselling Primer: Principles and Practice*. Monmouth: PCCS Books.

Dryden, W. (2021a). *Seven Principles of Single-Session Therapy*. London: Rationality Publications.

Dryden, W. (2021b). *Seven Principles of Doing Live Therapy Demonstrations.* London: Rationality Publications.

Dryden, W. (2021c). *Single-Session Therapy @ Onlinevents.* Sheffield: Onlinevents Publications.

Dryden, W. (2022a). *Single-Session Therapy: Responses to Frequently Asked Questions.* Abingdon: Routledge.

Dryden, W. (2022b). *Single-Session Integrated CBT (SSI-CBT): Distinctive Features.* 2nd edition. Abingdon: Routledge.

Dryden, W (2022c). *The SST Therapist's Pocket Companion.* London: Rationality Publications.

Dryden, W. (2023a). *ONEplus Therapy: Help at the Point of Need.* Sheffield: Onlinevents Publications.

Dryden, W. (2023b). *Single-Session Therapy and Regret.* Sheffield: Onlinevents Publications.

Dryden, W. (2024a). *How to Think and Intervene Like an REBT Therapist.* 2nd edition. Abingdon: Routledge.

Dryden, W. (2024b). *Single-Session Therapy: 100 Key Points and Techniques.* 2nd edition. Abingdon: Routledge.

Frank, J. D. (1961). *Persuasion and Healing: A Comprehensive Study of Psychotherapy.* Baltimore, MD: Johns Hopkins Press.

Giebelhausen, M. D., Robinson, S. G. & Cronin, J. J. (2011). Worth waiting for: Increasing satisfaction by making consumers wait. *Journal of the Academy of Marketing Science, 39,* 889–905.

Gyani, A., Shafran, R., Layard, R., & Clark, D. M. (2013). Enhancing recovery rates: Lessons from year one of IAPT. *Behaviour Research and Therapy, 51,* 597–606.

Hoyt, M. F. (2011). Foreword. In A. Slive & M. Bobele (Eds.), *When One Hour Is All You Have: Effective Therapy for Walk-In Clients* (pp. xix–xv). Phoenix, AZ: Zeig, Tucker & Theisen.

Hoyt, M. F. (2018). Single-session therapy: Stories, structures, themes, cautions, and prospects. In M. F. Hoyt, M. Bobele, A. Slive, J. Young & M. Talmon (Eds.), *Single-Session Therapy by Walk-In or Appointment: Administrative, Clinical, and Supervisory Aspects of One-at-a-Time Services* (pp. 155–174). New York: Routledge.

Hoyt, M. F., & Talmon, M. F. (2014). What the literature says: An annotated bibliography. In M. F. Hoyt & M. Talmon (Eds.), *Capturing the Moment: Single Session Therapy and Walk-In Services* (pp. 487–516). Bethel, CT: Crown House.

Hoyt, M. F., Young, J., & Rycroft, P. (2020). Single session thinking 2020. *Australian & New Zealand Journal of Family Therapy, 41*(3), 218–230.

Jones-Smith, E. (2014). *Strengths-Based Therapy: Connecting Theory, Practice and Skills.* Thousand Oaks, CA: Sage Publications.

Keller, G., & Papasan, J. (2012). *The One Thing: The Surprisingly Simple Truth Behind Extraordinary Results.* Austin, TX: Bard Press.

Mahrer, A. (Ed.). (1967). *The Goals of Psychotherapy.* Englewood Cliffs, NJ: Prentice Hall.

Norcross, J. C., & Cooper, M. (2021). *Personalizing Psychotherapy: Assessing and Accommodating Patient Preferences.* Washington, DC: American Psychological Association.

Pugh, M. (2019). *Cognitive Behavioural Chairwork: Distinctive Features.* Abingdon: Routledge.

Pugh, M. (2021). Single-session chairwork: Overview and case illustration of brief dialogical psychotherapy. *British Journal of Guidance & Counselling.* DOI: 10.1080/03069885.2021.1984395

Ratner, H., George, E., & Iveson, C. (2012). *Solution-Focused Brief Therapy; 100 Key Points and Techniques.* Hove: Routledge.

Seabury, B. A., Seabury, B. H., & Garvin, C. D. (2011). *Foundations of Interpersonal Practice in Social Work: Promoting Competence in Generalist Practice.* 3rd edition. Thousand Oaks, CA: Sage Publications.

Simon, G. E., Imel, Z. E., Ludman, E. J., & Steinfeld, B. J. (2012). Is dropout after a first psychotherapy visit always a bad outcome? *Psychiatric Services,* 63 (7), 705–707.

Snyder, T. A., & Barnett, J. E. (2006). Informed consent and the process of psychotherapy. *Psychotherapy Bulletin, 41,* 37–42.

Talmon, M. (1990). *Single Session Therapy: Maximizing the Effect of the First (and Often Only) Therapeutic Encounter.* San Francisco, CA: Jossey-Bass.

Tolle, E. (1999). *The Power of Now.* Novato, CA: New World Library.

Young, J. (2018). SST: The misunderstood gift that keeps on giving. In M. F. Hoyt, M. Bobele, A. Slive, J. Young & M. Talmon (Eds.), *Single-Session Therapy by Walk-In or Appointment: Administrative, Clinical, and Supervisory Aspects of One-at-a-Time Services* (pp. 40–58). New York: Routledge.

Young, J. (2024). *No Bullshit Therapy: How to Engage People Who Don't Want to Work with You.* Abingdon: Routledge.

Index

Note: Page numbers in **bold** denote tables.

Acceptance and Commitment
  Therapy (ACT) 128
action plans 37, 156–162
applicant role 22
appointments 6, 10–11, 23, 68
assessment 10–11, 12, 13, 20–22,
  38–39
attitude change solutions 127–128

Barnett, J. E. 65, 66
beginning the session 23, 83–92, **84**;
  informed consent 65–67, 84–86;
  problem focus 90–92; purpose
  focus 88–90; using pre-session
  questionnaire 86–87
behavioural change solutions 129
Bion, Wilfred 17
bonds, in working alliance 33–34
Bouverie Centre, Melbourne,
  Australia 169

case discussion 74–76
case history 11, 13
chairwork 155
client feedback 24, 168–170, 173–178
client goals: problem-related 35–36,
  93, 157, 158, 162; session 35–36,
  41, 93–95
'client-led' principle 25–26, 38–43
client role 22
'client suitability' question 25–28,
  38–39
client–therapist relationship 23,
  33–37, 65, 100

complex problems 32
confidentiality 34, 66
consent, informed 65–67, 84–86
contracts 6, 66, 67, 171–172
conventional therapy mindset 1, 2, 5,
  7, 64; assessment 11, 13, 20–22,
  38–39; client goals 41; 'client-led'
  principle 38–39, 40–41, 42–43;
  'client suitability' question 25–28,
  38–39; 'dropping out' 21–22, 41,
  50; first session 20–22; focus on
  disorders 29–32, 40–41; 'help at
  the point of need' principle 11,
  13–15; 'less is more' principle 49;
  'power of now' principle 44,
  46–47; prior knowledge of
  clients 16, 18–19; process 24; risk
  13–14; working alliance 37

disorders 29–32, 40–41, 62–63
'dropping out' 21–22, 41, 50
duration of therapy *see* therapy length

embedding solutions 148–149
ending the session 24, 163–167;
  further help options 42, 164–165;
  generalising the solution 164;
  'hit it and quit it' principle 77;
  informing clients about 57,
  58; last-minute questions and
  statements 165–166; session
  summaries 163–164; takeaways
  164
enquirer role 22

explorer role 22
external resources 131–132

feedback 24, 168–170, 173–178
focus, creating and maintaining
    103–107
follow-up 24, 168–170, 173–178
Frank, Jerome 163
further help options 42, 164–165, 169

'gateway' approach 39, 42
generalising solutions 164
goals: problem-related 35–36, 93,
    157, 158, 162; session 35–36, 41,
    93–95
guiding principles 134
Gyani, A. 5, 21

'help at the point of need' principle
    9–15
help-related roles 22
helping stances 36–37, 96–102
'hit it and quit it' principle 77
homework assignments 156–157
Hoyt, Michael 8, 22, 41–42, 44–45

imagery 153–155
Improving Access to Psychological
    Therapy (IAPT) services 5,
    21–22, 25, 38–39
'in-session' thinking see SST
    'in-session' thinking
inference change solutions 128
information for potential clients 55–59
informed consent 65–67, 84–86
internal strengths 130–131, 158–159
interrupting clients 104–105

leaflets, information for potential
    clients 58–59
'less is more' principle 48–49,
    77–78
'let the client's brain take the strain'
    principle 78–79

'One-At-A-Time' therapy (OAATT)
    8, 10, 29

ONEplus therapy 8; contract 66,
    67, 171–172; information for
    potential clients 55–59; post-
    session follow-up 170, 173–178;
    pre-session questionnaire 56–57,
    69–73; questions from potential
    clients 60–64
'open-access, enter now' services
    10, 16, 23, 26, 40, 68
'orientation' thinking see SST
    'orientation' thinking

peer support 76
post-session follow-up 24, 168–170,
    173–178
'power of now' principle 44–47
'pre-session' thinking see SST
    'pre-session' thinking
prior knowledge of clients 16–19
problem-maintenance factors
    119–126, **120**; using opposites to
    142–143, **144–145**
problem-related goals 35–36, 93,
    157, 158, 162
problems 108–126; beginning the
    session with focus on 90–92;
    client's unwitting maintenance
    of 119–126, **120**; client's view of
    108–110; complex 32; exceptions
    to 136–138; helping stances
    36–37, 96–102; identifying
    nominated 93–95; prior attempts
    to solve 135–136; therapy-
    informed view of 111–112;
    understanding in context 112–117;
    working with specific example of
    117–119; see also solutions
psychotherapy, definition 20–21

questionnaires, pre-session 16–17,
    23, 56–57, 68–73, 79–80, 86–87
questions: last-minute 165–166;
    from potential clients 60–64

Ratner, H. 136
recordings of sessions 63, 76
reframing solutions 127

rehearsing solutions 37, 150–155
resources, external 131–132
risk 13–14, 63
role models 132–134
roleplay 150–153
roles, help-related 22
Rosenbaum, Robert 44–45

session goals 35–36, 41, 93–95
session summaries 163–164
sessions 23–24; action plans 37,
156–162; chairwork 155; creating
and maintaining focus 103–107;
helping stances 36–37, 96–102;
imagery 153–155; interrupting
clients 104–105; 'less is more'
principle 48–49, 77–78; 'let the
client's brain take the strain'
principle 78–79; recording and
transcripts 63, 76; roleplay
150–153; session goals 35–36,
41, 93–95; working without prior
knowledge of client 16–19;
see also beginning the session;
ending the session; problems;
solutions
single-session therapy (SST): by
appointment 6, 10–11, 23, 68;
'client suitability' question 25–28,
38–39; definition 6; 'open-access,
enter now' services 10, 16, 23, 26,
40, 68; process overview 22–24,
62; working alliance 23, 33–37,
65, 100; see also SST 'in-session'
thinking; SST 'orientation'
thinking; SST 'pre-session'
thinking
situational change solutions 129
solutions 127–149; action plans 37,
156–162; attitude change
127–128; behavioural change
129; changing client's relationship
to problem 128–129; to complex
problems 32; embedding
148–149; generalising 164;
inference change 128; reframing
127; rehearsing 37, 150–155;

situational change 129; types of
127–129; using exceptions to
problem 136–138; using external
resources 131–132; using guiding
principles 134; using instances
of goal occurring 138–141; using
internal strengths 130–131; using
opposites to problem-maintenance
factors 142–143, **144–145**; using
prior attempts 135–136; using
role models 132–134; using
shared understanding of problem
145–147
SST by appointment 6, 10–11, 23,
68
SST 'in-session' thinking 3, 81;
action plans 37, 156–162; creating
and maintaining focus 103–107;
helping stances 36–37, 96–102;
interrupting clients 104–105; 'less
is more' principle 48–49, 77–78;
'let the client's brain take the
strain' principle 78–79; session
goals 35–36, 41, 93–95; working
without prior knowledge of
client 16–19; see also beginning
the session; ending the session;
problems; solutions
SST 'orientation' thinking 3; 'first
session as complete in itself'
20–24; 'focus on the person, not
the disorder' 29–32, 40–41; 'help
at the point of need' principle
9–15; 'less is more' principle
48–49, 77–78; 'one or more
sessions are possible' 5–8, 12;
'potentially anyone can be helped
in a session' 25–28; 'power of
now' principle 44–47; 'SST
is client-led' principle 25–26,
38–43; 'take nothing for granted'
principle 50–51; 'working alliance
can be established rapidly' 33–37;
'working without prior knowledge
of client is possible' 16–19
SST 'pre-session' thinking 3,
22–23, 53; case discussion 74–76;

contracts 6, 66, 67, 171–172; difficulties with SST 77–79; help-related roles 22; information for potential clients 55–59; informed consent 65–67, 84–86; listening to recordings 76; peer support 76; pre-session questionnaires 16–17, 23, 56–57, 68–73, 79–80, 86–87; pre-session telephone calls 56–57; questions from potential clients 60–64; supervision 74–76; therapist preparation 74–79
strengths, internal 130–131, 158–159
substance misuse 123–124
summaries 163–164
supervision 74–76

'take nothing for granted' principle 50–51
takeaways 164

Talmon, Moshe 21, 44–45, 50
tasks 36–37
telephone calls: post-session follow-up 169, 170, 175–178; pre-session 56–57
therapy length 5–8; client choice 14, 41–42; client satisfaction with one session 39, 42, 50; 'dropping out' 21–22, 41, 50; modal number of sessions 12, 22, 41–42
Tolle, Eckhart 44
transcripts of sessions 63

views, in working alliance 34–35

waiting lists 6, 9–10
'walk-in' services see 'open-access, enter now' services
websites, information for potential clients 55–57
working alliance 23, 33–37, 65, 100

For Product Safety Concerns and Information please contact our EU representative GPSR@taylorandfrancis.com Taylor & Francis Verlag GmbH, Kaufingerstraße 24, 80331 München, Germany

Printed and bound by CPI Group (UK) Ltd, Croydon, CR0 4YY

08/06/2025

01897005-0002